"Sue Sanders offers a double delight: fresh, trenchant advice for parents fearing the 'terrible tweens,' and a moving family portrait. Hard-earned wit and wisdom can be found on each and every page."

—LINDA KEENAN, author of *Suburgatory*, the title behind the ABC sitcom

"Sue Sanders has been there, answered that, and figured out what matters most to kids and parents. (Hint: Honesty and humor loom large.)"

—LENORE SKENAZY, author of the book and blog *Free-Range Kids*

"*Mom, I'm Not a Kid Anymore* should be handed out to parents at every middle school orientation meeting. It's filled with the stuff parents whisper to each other—or keep to themselves—when it comes to raising young teens. Sue Sanders (and her daughter Lizzie) provide a common sense guide to the conversations you'll navigate through middle school and beyond."

—JEN SINGER, MommaSaid.net, author of *You're a Good Mom (and Your Kids Aren't So Bad Either)*

"Compulsively readable, heartfelt, and funny, this book is a savvy best friend I will turn to again and again as my kids grow up. Sanders deftly aces the dance all parents engage in when counseling their kids about the rites of passage of adolescence—and her transparency regarding her own hair-raising youthful shenanigans is a welcome tonic of 'real' seldom found in this genre."

—CANDACE WALSH, author of *Licking the Spoon: A Memoir of Food, Family, and Identity*

THE EXPERIMENT

"A fun and often astute look at the ways that our teenage children drive us mad and to a new place of clarity. Sanders offers real answers on how to get through the looking glass of our children all in one piece."
—SUZANNE FINNAMORE, bestselling author of
Otherwise Engaged and *Split*

"Sanders deeply engages with all the sticky (and some of the most heartening) situations of parenting a young adult. She guides us through terra incognita with grace, wit, compassion, and a whole lot of smarts. Her compass is true."
—MELISSA HOLBROOK PIERSON, author of
The Perfect Vehicle and *The Place You Love Is Gone*

MOM,
I'M NOT A KID
ANYMORE

NAVIGATING
25 INEVITABLE
CONVERSATIONS
THAT ARRIVE BEFORE
YOU KNOW IT

SUE SANDERS

THE EXPERIMENT
NEW YORK

To Lizzie and Jeff,
my "official" family.

CONTENTS

Introduction   ix

PART 1
"MOM, HAVE YOU EVER SMOKED MARIJUANA?"
(expected, but still surprising conversations)   1

> "Mom, have you ever smoked marijuana?"   3
>
> "I got my period in Learning Lab!"   7
>
> "Tell me about your mean girl."   13
>
> "You and Dad do that?"   21
>
> "Damn it." / "Did she just say what I think she did?"   26
>
> "Will we be an official family?"   31
>
> "What if I don't make any friends?"   39
>
> "Anna's brother got his learner's permit."   47
>
> "Will she be okay at camp?"   55
>
> "I'm angry at you!"   61
>
> "You're not my boss." / "Go to your room."   68

PART 2
"AREN'T FAMILY VALUES A GOOD THING?"
(modern family talk)   71

> "Aren't family values a good thing?"   73
>
> "Lizzie wants to be friends on Facebook."   79

"Do you believe in God?" 85

"Can I get American Eagle jeans?" 91

"How do you type on this thing?" / "Here, let me try." 98

"Do these shorts make my butt look big?" 101

"Do you drink wine every night?" 109

"They told me they needed space." 117

"You wouldn't understand." / "Try me." 125

"I got a 3 on my essay." 129

PART 3
"MOM, I'M NOT A KID ANYMORE."
(and everything in between) 137

"Mom, I'm not a kid anymore." 139

"What kind of question is this?" 145

"Please, please can we go?" 153

"How was your trip to Mount St. Helens?" / "It was, like, awesome!" 160

"What did he say?" 165

"Telephone for you, Lizzie." 173

"Where's the rest of this dress?" 181

"They're having tryouts next week!" 187

"Will the world be around when I have kids?" 197

"I'm making a list." / "Of what?" 202

Acknowledgments 207

INTRODUCTION

Parenting a preteen can be a bit like trudging up a dune in the Mojave. As soon as you think you're on firm ground, the sands slip, leaving you wondering where you stand. When my daughter, Lizzie, was younger, I had many parent friends—both close and casual—to talk with about whatever child-rearing issue of the day left me slightly off-kilter. But as she grew older, the support group dwindled. Some friends moved, others went back to work. Or we just drifted apart. The social glue that had bonded us was our young children, and now that they were older, those ties dissolved.

Even among my remaining mom friends, when we did manage to find the time for a coffee or a glass of wine, our conversation began to veer from kid-centric topics to adult ones. It was as if we'd left our parent talk on the playground once our children had outgrown slides and sandboxes. We still chatted about school issues occasionally, but more often we wanted to find out about one another's lives.

It wasn't that long ago that I was once very motivated to reach out to other mothers. My marriage had ended shortly after Lizzie turned three, and as a full-time single mother I was desperate to talk to people over three feet tall about parenting issues and pretty much everything else. My ex-husband,

Mike, and I had been together since college, and thirteen years into our eighteen-year relationship, he developed a severe case of bipolar disorder. When he took his medication, he was the man I'd fallen in love with; but he'd often refuse to do so and then change into a stranger. After five years and more than a few frightening incidents, I took Lizzie and left. Eventually, I started dating and met the wonderful man who'd become my second husband—and a co-parent who Lizzie sometimes calls by name and sometimes calls Dad.

The summer before Lizzie started sixth grade, our family moved across the country, from upstate New York to Portland, Oregon. My closest friends in Portland have children far older or far younger than Lizzie, and it was more difficult to connect with parents of children her age than it had been when she was smaller. Back then, no one thought it odd to ask a total stranger what to do about a parenting challenge—or, if asked, to offer advice. How did they get their preschoolers to stop whining? Had my daughter ever announced she was never going to eat anything green again? Did their eight-year-olds have a fiendishly difficult time with spelling the way mine did?

Middle school is a whole new playing field, for Lizzie—and me. As a young teen, Lizzie's life is more distinct from mine—she is more independent. When I pick her up at school, I see other parents and smile at them, but they're sitting in their cars, often texting or reading e-mail. On the occasions when we do speak with one another, such as at school functions and holiday music festivals, conversations are limited to small talk. I'm not going to place my pasta salad on the table at the back-to-school potluck, turn to the stranger next to me, and inquire whether her twelve-year-old had recently asked if she'd ever smoked pot.

We're not sharing these experiences with one another as parents—but perhaps we should be. By speaking with other parents to find out how they handled dilemmas, we can get a perspective different from our own. Maybe your thirteen-year-old just asked if you had been bullied when you were a kid, or your twelve-year-old jumped in the car after school one day and excitedly told you she just got her period. Whatever the event, it's good to hear what others did. Although my MA in education helped me notice which behaviors were developmentally appropriate when Lizzie was younger, the degree goes only so far. No textbook covers what to do when your child comes home from school crying because she had been excluded from trick-or-treating by kids she thought were her friends.

I don't pretend to have all the answers. Actually, other than "Why?" and "Are we there yet?" I couldn't have anticipated many of the questions that seem to have been lobbed at me like a surprise attack over the past few years, now that Lizzie is fourteen. I like to think that reading these tales is a bit like the advice you get from a friend over coffee: perhaps you agree on some aspects of parenting, maybe you disagree on others, but it's still good to hear from someone who is going through something similar.

This is an especially challenging age, one that's filled with an abundance of drama, including Oscar-worthy eye rolls, deep sighs, and cries of "You don't understand!" And that's just child-parent dynamics. The child-child drama is set on an entirely different stage, one that to young teens can seem larger than the Metropolitan Opera's.

Over the years, I have learned a few basic lessons, though, about how to deal with an emerging teenager. To summarize:

- **Hold on to your sense of humor—and don't let go.** It comes in handy during such parent and preteen classics as the "sex talk" and the near constant refrain, "No, you can't do [insert ridiculous request of the day], even if everyone else is allowed."

- **Trust your gut—you already know far more than you may think you do.** Experts have their place, but common sense is too often underrated.

- **Answer your child's questions honestly—even if it's uncomfortable.** Adolescents seem to come equipped with inborn lie detectors. They know when you're bending the truth. That doesn't mean you have to give an unvarnished version of events or that you shouldn't give the truth a bit of a spin. When my daughter asked if I'd ever smoked marijuana as a teenager, I told her I had. (I just didn't tell her that several years of high school were spent in a pot-shrouded haze.)

- **We don't parent in a vacuum—it's more like when a pebble is chucked gently into a pond.** There's a ripple effect of how we were raised that, directly or indirectly, consciously or unconsciously, affects how we bring up our own kids. I've found that if you hated middle school, it can feel a bit like reliving it all over again when you see your child face a challenge. For me, all those feelings of rejection, which had seemed as mercifully forgotten as the permed hair of the seventies, come rushing out of some emotional recess. Everyone carries a bit of their past into their kids' present. I try to make sure I'm not lugging giant, overstuffed baggage. Sometimes I find it necessary to stop, take a breath, and tell myself (once again), "This is my issue, not Lizzie's."

And so I bring all this into the foreground while raising Lizzie. We talk frequently about many subjects—from puberty to politics, from her class trip to Mount St. Helens to mean girls, openly and honestly, often over her favorite drink: café mocha without the espresso. I hope that by laying the bedrock brick by brick through genuine communication, it will make things easier as she gets older. I also believe it will help her make good choices when she's an adult. And I hope that one day, if and when Lizzie has children (in the distant future), she'll continue the conversation, speaking candidly with them. Because a strong foundation, built with direct talk, can withstand the seismic force of millions of rolled eyes.

"MOM, HAVE YOU EVER SMOKED MARIJUANA?"

(expected, but still surprising conversations)

"MOM, HAVE YOU EVER SMOKED MARIJUANA?"

Mom, have you ever smoked marijuana?" my eleven-year-old daughter, Lizzie, asked as we pulled up in our driveway, gravel crunching under the car's wheels. Her question wasn't totally out of the blue—we'd just passed a passel of teenagers hanging out on our town's main street, a smoky cloud hovering over them, and my husband, Jeff, and I had commented about the local drug problem—but I was still caught off guard. Jeff muttered something unintelligible and darted from the car to let the dog out of the house since he'd been cooped up all day. I sat, frozen with sudden panic.

Do I answer honestly? Or lie? Spinning possible answers like a roulette wheel in my mind, I opted for truth.

"Yes, I did. A long time ago, in high school." I unclasped my seat belt and turned around to face her.

"Why?" Lizzie actually gasped. She's the type of kid who likes rules, the more of them the better. For now, anyway, there are few hints of the adolescent rebel I'm sure is lurking inside her somewhere. (She's also the type of kid who uses words like "marijuana" instead of "pot.")

Why indeed? I'd been curious about it, but I also wanted, desperately, to escape my social incompetence, the discomfort of living in a small southern town where I felt like an outcast. The town fit me as well as the Calvin Klein jeans I wore, so tight and claustrophobic that I had to lie down on my bed, inhale, close my eyes, and will myself smaller to zip them up. In pure rebel mode, I quickly became eager to see exactly what I could get away with. Quite a lot, I discovered.

Pot was a social lubricant that greased my rusty social skills: the ritual of rolling a joint and passing it around a room of kids my own age was a common currency I could pull out of my pocket and use anywhere. Plus, pot made my eight-track tapes sound really great. As an added bonus, it was something forbidden and illegal—and sure to horrify my straitlaced parents.

Of course, I wasn't going to tell Lizzie all this. I wanted to bare my soul, but not get totally naked. I wanted to be candid with her, but not too much so—my candor would be rated PG. So I simply told her I'd been curious. However, I cautioned, way back then (during my own personal stone age), marijuana wasn't as strong as it is now and drug laws were different. Now, kids can ruin their chances of getting into college or attaining a scholarship if they're caught with drugs. And even at eleven, Lizzie takes the concept of college very seriously. She plans to study writing and cooking. This week, at least. (Not long ago she wanted to be an elf.)

Shocked, Lizzie rushed into the house and raced over to her dad, shouting, "Did you know Mom smoked marijuana in high school?" He did.

Like many other parenting challenges, this one thwacked me in the face when I wasn't expecting it. I'd been meaning to talk with Lizzie about drugs; I really had. But I'd just never got around to it. Sure, I'd read articles about what you're supposed to do. Then I'd forget, or get busy folding laundry, or my e-mail would "ding." There never seemed to be a right time or a spare minute to bring up the subject. Or perhaps I just sank into my cocoon of denial and avoidance, waiting for the perfect opportunity, the right teachable moment, to present itself. But it never did. All the teachable moments seemed to have played hooky.

Lizzie and I had snuggled together and talked a little more about drugs—I'd asked her if she had any more questions, and she did:

"Weren't you worried about going to jail?"

"Isn't smoking marijuana bad for you, like you can get lung cancer and stuff?"

"Do you do it now?"

Later, after she was tucked in bed, I searched the Internet for parenting advice and I discovered I'd apparently done everything all wrong. I was supposed to bring up the subject of drugs way back when my sixth grader was still in preschool, finger painting and sorting colorful plastic toy bears into muffin tins. I should have discussed "good drugs" versus "bad drugs" with her when I gave her a Children's Tylenol or Motrin for her fever. Briefly feeling like a failure, I berated myself for not reading more parenting books when Lizzie was younger. Although these guides may have their place, I'd often felt it was as kindling. I've never been a big fan of "experts" telling me what to do—a residual healthy distrust of authority from my adolescence. For the first time, though, I wondered if forgoing all of this reading meant that I had missed the basic steps of parenting. Was I simply Doing It Wrong?

Closing the parenting website that night after Lizzie had asked if I'd tried marijuana, I decided to rely on my most trusted source of parenting advice: my friends. I opened Facebook and posted a status update, a query, asking friends who both had children *and* had inhaled how they'd talked to their kids about drugs. The postings poured in. Most said they favored being honest about their history and discussing the legal and health ramifications over any sort of *Reefer Madness* fear-inducing fervor or any type of hardline demand of "Don't ever do it." Back in high school, I'd been on the receiving end of "Don't ever do it." I didn't "Don't ever do it" quite a lot.

So I will continue to listen to Lizzie. Once I'd answered her questions about marijuana the night she'd asked if I'd tried it, she appeared satisfied and she didn't bring up the topic again for a long time. But other questions keep coming—including those that seem to arrive out of nowhere.

A few months later, while I was having lunch, Lizzie came into the dining room, face furrowed, and asked, "What's a virgin?" Nearly choking on my seltzer, I asked what she meant. She went into the kitchen and came back with a container and pointed. "It says right here: virgin lemonade."

"I GOT MY PERIOD IN LEARNING LAB!"

Guess what?" Lizzie said, leaning through the car's open window after school one afternoon, practically vibrating with excitement. Without waiting for an answer, she tossed her backpack in the car and jumped into the front seat, blurting, "I got my period today in Learning Lab!"

"Congratulations! That's big news!" I said, and asked what happened.

"I could feel something squishy in my underwear and told my teacher. She gave me a pad and let me and Sara go to the bathroom. We couldn't stop laughing. Can I tell Jeff as soon as we get home?" Lizzie said, gleefully.

I assured her she could tell her dad and asked where she wanted to go that night for dinner to celebrate. Lizzie and I had been talking about puberty for the previous few years, and she was thrilled to finally get her period.

This was very different from my own experience.

During the summer between seventh and eighth grades, my period arrived one day without warning, like a surprise houseguest. My mom had never discussed menstruation with me, but I knew exactly what the dark red stains in my underwear were, thanks only to overhearing girls' gossip earlier that year during gym class. This was possibly the most useful thing I learned in phys ed that year—I'm still baffled by the rules of volleyball.

Having been educated by teenage girls in polyester uniforms, I knew that "Auntie Flo" had arrived. I simply stuffed toilet paper in my underpants and pulled them up.

I was unsure what to say to my mom, so I just stood awkwardly outside her craft room as her sewing machine whirred, wondering if it was possible for a thirteen-year-old to spontaneously combust from embarrassment. But my mom figured out exactly what had happened before I was able to say anything—which was lucky for me, since I seemed incapable of forming a coherent sentence. She translated my, "I, uh, uh . . ." into something along the lines of, "Mother, I got my very first period today and I'm a bit unsure about what to do next." She gave me a self-conscious smile, got up from her chair, and told me to follow her. In her bedroom, she slid open her closet door (was this where she kept menstrual supplies?), pulled out a mysterious box from the top shelf, and handed it to me. Inside was a smaller box of maxi pads and a booklet about menstruation. After showing me exactly what to do with the pad, she disappeared back into her sewing room, and as a new "woman," I read about my period, alone. I don't think the words *period* or *menstruation* were ever mentioned in our house. My mom seemed even more uncomfortable with my changing body than I was.

It wasn't too surprising that she didn't talk about my period with me. She was the oldest of nine children, the only girl in practically a baseball team of little brothers. She grew up in a small agricultural town (Fillmore, Missouri, population about two hundred), in a white clapboard farmhouse with one bathroom. I've often wondered what her childhood was like—and how much of it was truly a childhood. I suspect there wasn't much time for my grandmother to sit down with her for a chat about puberty. There probably wasn't a whole lot of time to sit down at all, with a constant pile of diapers to change and wash, babies to feed, farm chores to do. Besides, back then puberty and sexuality weren't discussed—this was parenting's Silent Generation. After I started my period, though my mom and I never talked about it, somehow new supplies just seemed to magically appear under the bathroom sink in a never-ending, regenerating stockpile.

* * *

I wanted Lizzie's experience to be different. Our family had always been fairly open, talking factually about the body as the occasions arose. When Lizzie was three, we shared a stall in public bathrooms, where she saw me change sanitary pads. She was also fascinated by tampons, often asking loudly, "Mommy, you need tompans?" I did make her turn around for a second if I had to change a tampon with a, "Hey, look over there!" I didn't want her to think it was okay to stick things in her vagina. It was bad enough when her two-year-old friend had to go to the doctor because he stuck raisins up his nose; I didn't want to ever have to worry about explaining to the pediatrician that my daughter had been playing "tompan."

When she was in fourth grade, we got to talk more earnestly about puberty.

It all started with Judy Blume. "Mom, what's a period?" Lizzie asked, with *Are You There God? It's Me,*

Margaret. folded flat against her ten-year-old chest as she sprawled on the sofa. I told her and reminded her of the pads she'd occasionally seen me use. "Why do all the girls want *that?*" she asked, shocked. I studied the carpet, unsure exactly what to say, hoping the answer would suddenly materialize among its geometric patterns. I muttered something about how girls think getting their period makes them more grown up. "Is it like a bloody nose? I don't like those," she said, shuddering slightly. This was true. Her response to a few drops of blood trickling from a nostril made me think she was being bludgeoned.

So, back in fourth grade, we had our first "serious" talk about puberty. Conversations take two people, though. My daughter chattered away happily, but somehow I was whisked back in time, morphing into an embarrassed adolescent—or maybe her mother. I felt my mom's discomfort in every cell. It would have been easy to give Lizzie a pamphlet or book to read on her own, but I *couldn't* not talk about puberty. I needed to talk. I decided I could use a little help, though—perhaps a book that Lizzie and I could read together and talk about and then she could keep in her room to reread, when and if she wanted. I went online and posted a note on my local parenting bulletin board, asking for recommendations on books about puberty for my daughter's then demographic, the unfortunately named "tween" girls. I then went to Amazon and read reviews of a few of the suggested books. The following day while my daughter was at school, I picked up a copy of *The Care & Keeping of You* at our local bookstore. That night at story time, propped up on pillows in Lizzie's bed, we took turns reading it. Lizzie was especially interested in the chapter about how her body would change in the coming years and carefully studied the illustrations that showed the different stages her breasts would go through. Suddenly, she sat up straight, as though she'd been snapped to attention, and unzipped her one-piece footed fleece pajamas. "I'm at stage two!" she cried out, gleefully exposing her developing breasts, while I realized that I was still uneasy about discussing puberty.

Why did I feel uncomfortable talking to *my* daughter about her changing body and emerging sexuality? Was I once again thinking about *my* childhood instead of hers, something I've vowed not to do many times but still can't seem to help doing? I grew up not knowing what to expect— from developing breasts to getting my period to, later, having teenage sex and getting pregnant. I wanted to be sure Lizzie would know what was happening to her. Through information, she would be prepared for whatever might lie ahead. Still, the memories of my own adolescence haunted me, adding to my discomfort about speaking frankly.

But here's the funny thing: Lizzie seemed to feel comfortable commenting on anything and everything we read. She was genuinely curious and wanted to know all there was to know about her changing body. Lizzie and I kept talking and plowed blindly ahead, and suddenly periods and puberty weren't so scary. They were exciting.

"Girls are so lucky. We get all the best stuff like tampons and periods and bras!"

"Shaving your legs looks scary. I don't think I'll do that."

"Can I feel your breasts?" Without waiting for a reply, she reached out with one hand. "Wow, yours are big. Definitely stage five."

To Lizzie, puberty was just something else to chat about, as natural as discussing Harry Potter or soccer practice.

A few days after we'd read the book together, Lizzie approached me with a worried look. She held the book out to me, a page carefully marked with a purple smiling monkey

Post-it note. As she held it out to me like a silver chalice, she whispered, "I think it's happening." I flipped open the book to the marked page, which was all about getting a period.

"You're getting your period?" I tried not to sound too doubtful, since she'd just turned ten.

With an extremely serious expression, she silently tapped the line "Some girls get moody or irritable right before they get their periods." She looked up, eyes wide as saucers.

"You're feeling moody and irritable?" I asked.

She nodded, paused, then asked, "What does irritable mean?"

I told Lizzie she'd get her period as soon as her body was ready.

And sure enough, a little less than three years later, her body was ready. I'm glad we paved the way with puberty talk. It made Lizzie excited to share the news of her first period. We went out for Vietnamese that night, eating plates full of chili noodles and clinking our glasses together, quietly toasting, "To firsts!" After all, she might be comfortable talking to us about her period, but she was still a self-conscious adolescent, and one who would have been (justifiably) horrified if we'd toasted, "To first periods!"

Instead of "Auntie Flo," Lizzie decided to call hers a dot. ("You know, a period is the dot at the end of a sentence.") She was still learning, though. As we were clearing dinner dishes from the table several days later, she asked, "Mom, when do women stop getting their periods?" I told her in their mid- to late forties or fifties. A look of alarm spread across her face. "I'm going to have to wear a pad every day until then?" she cried. Attempting to keep a serious expression, I assured her this wasn't so.

A week before I started seventh grade, my family moved for the thirteenth time. My dad was in the oil business, so after three years of living in one place, we left Indonesia, where I'd had friends, for a small southern town, where I had none.

In Indonesia, my best friend, Anne, and I made up secret languages, wrote notes to each other in lemon juice "invisible ink," and solved a series of mysteries. We wrote stories and built Sioux villages from cardboard boxes and tape. We baked a cake from scratch, lifting the mixer from the bowl before we'd turned it off, splattering batter everywhere, and transforming the kitchen in a Jackson Pollock–like work. I'd meet Anne and my friends Karen or Lisa at the American Club's pool, where we'd spend hours playing Marco Polo or doing cannonballs from the diving board.

In Louisiana, I didn't fit in with the other seventh-grade girls, but I connected with another misfit. We had virtually nothing in common but were drawn together by a desire to not be alone. We didn't live near each other or have many classes together but met for lunch each day and hid in the

13

home ec building's nook, avoiding the lunchroom, a large room filled with tables populated by clusters of children who either ignored us and talked through us as if we didn't exist or mocked our clothing choices with, "Oh, I just *love* your shirts." My only companion dressed exclusively in navy culottes and white button-down shirts, her wardrobe compliments of her evangelical Pentecostal religion. We were practically the only two girls without the Hairdo: a Farrah Fawcett cut that necessitated a cloud of Aqua Net hair spray to protect it from Louisiana's humidity.

Each morning I took the bus to school, and each morning I was bullied by a girl I'll call Jane. She latched on to me shortly after the school year began. I had new school supplies: blue Bic pens, college-lined paper, and a doodle-free Mead Trapper Keeper. She had a new target: me.

"Ew—don't you wash your hair?" Jane shouted at me from two rows back as her sidekick, Kim, laughed. I did wash my hair, but apparently not enough. Jane didn't make fun of just my hair. A pimple on my chin earned a belligerent, "Oh, gross! That's disgusting!" Possibly because Jane was one of those girls who always wore the "right" clothes, undoubtedly purchased at the town's only boutique, my taste in outfits seemed to especially annoy her.

"*What* are you wearing?" she said, sneering at my Pepto-pink overalls.

They were very pink.

I wasn't exactly the most fashion-conscious kid. In fact, I was pretty much fashion unconscious—to the point where I could have used some smelling salts and a personal shopper.

After weeks of trying to ignore her—and everyone else ignoring us, probably relieved she was picking on me rather than them—I made sure that I sat behind the bus driver. I thought sitting behind him would protect me. Instead, he just turned up the volume on the Eagles. (Years before Noriega was tortured by rock 'n' roll music, so was I.) This went on all through seventh grade. That year, I pretended to be sick so often that I'm surprised my parents didn't whisk me off to the local hospital. Of course, I didn't tell anyone what was happening. I thought if I ignored it hard enough, it would go away. I repeated, silently but over and over, *Sticks and stones may break my bones, but words will never hurt me.* But they did. So I just went more inside myself.

*   *   *

Eighth grade, I decided early on, would be different! I waited for the bus on the first day of school wearing a maroon skirt and polyester beige shirt printed with cowboy hats and horses. I'd picked it out on a back-to-school shopping expedition to Sears. I was proud of the way the outfit matched, thinking it was a perfect look for a sophisticated eighth grader. And now that I was in my last year of junior high, I was, by default, sophisticated. I looked great! Until the moment I boarded the bus, and Jane and Kim started to neigh. It was clear that eighth grade was going to be just like seventh—only with bigger breasts.

Even though it's been more than three decades since I rode that bus to middle school, I've been thinking a lot about it lately. Lizzie recently started seventh grade, and I see my old social awkwardness reflected in her. Although she's met her share of bullies in previous years, middle school girls are different. They take bullying to new highs (and lows). There's overt cruelty, shunning someone like an excommunicated Amish, and the kinds of mind games that would make Machiavelli cringe. Toss in technology with their newfound freedom and independence and it's a wicked brew, one that makes the kindergarten threat of "You can't come to my birthday party!" seem charming.

But there's an added challenge with Lizzie in middle school: I'm spirited back to junior high and become, emotionally, thirteen again. I have to constantly remind myself that she's not me and that she handles mean girls differently from the way I did. Also, while back at my school they practically taught kids how to bully, Lizzie attends a school with a no-bullying policy and teachers who help kids work though social dynamics. She feels safe telling someone they made her feel bad. And she also feels comfortable—for now, anyway—talking to her dad and me if she ever feels excluded. But when a girl sends Lizzie a vicious e-mail, uninviting her from a much-anticipated Halloween group outing, I'm right back on that school bus.

"Lana told me they didn't want me to go trick-or-treating with them," Lizzie said quietly after receiving the e-mail. She blinked rapidly. "Lana said maybe I could go next year."

I hugged Lizzie and secretly hoped Lana would get a stomachache from too much Halloween candy.

That night, while I was trying (and failing) to keep my stuff separate from Lizzie's, my husband gently suggested I try to find Jane. Maybe it would help ease my own pain and prevent me from imposing my own past on my daughter's present. Actually, I had talked to Jane about it one time—in eleventh grade. I had bumped into her at a Catholic school I briefly attended while on temporary suspension from the public school for getting caught smoking pot. As we shared a cigarette behind a bus during recess, away from the nuns' prying eyes, I asked why she'd picked on me mercilessly and why she'd been so mean back in junior high. She studied the ground and flicked an ash. She didn't answer but looked embarrassed. A bell rang and we went back to class, matter dropped.

Thirty-five years later, I have a family and a profession that I love. I'm happy, healthy, and (most of the time, anyway) well-adjusted. I have wonderful friends. Still, when I looked Jane up on Facebook and sent her a note, I reverted back to my old teenage self, shyly suggesting that I was sure she wouldn't remember me, but could I ask her a few questions.

An hour later, I heard back. I was right. She didn't remember me but said she was interested to hear more and that she'd try to answer any questions I had. I responded that I'd hated middle school and now that my daughter was that age, I was sifting through memories and trying to sort the then-versus-now and see how it all fit together. I asked if she remembered the bus ride to junior high school. I was honestly curious if she had any recollection of it. Middle schoolers assume they're living under a giant spotlight and that everyone is watching their every move. But although she didn't remember me, she definitely recalled being cruel.

"Oh yes, I was the mean girl," she wrote. "No doubt. When we shared the cigarette (I can't believe you remember that!), I'm hoping I was embarrassed and was on my way to changing. But I did change—when I went to college and met *really* mean girls."

When I asked Jane why she'd been like that, she said she thought it came down to three reasons. She'd felt an enormous sense of entitlement. "My mom put me up on a pedestal and I was told I was special, so I acted special and better than others." She'd come from a family of huge personalities and, as she put it, "I was an attention whore—positive or negative." And it turned out she'd been bullied herself in fifth grade. "My bully was brutal and the police had to get involved. That kid took a lot from me emotionally, physically, and materially. He actually ended up much later going to prison for murder. And I know what you're thinking—if I was bullied, why would I become one? Because if I was mean first, then others would be afraid of me, not the other way around.

"I just wish I'd known back in middle school what I know now, but we both know that's not how life works. I'm sorry I made fun of you and your hair and made the bus ride a nightmare. I'm sure today we'd both enjoy each other's company—well, I hope you'd like me!"

So what about me; why hadn't I stood up to Jane in junior high? I didn't have a BULLY ME! sign taped to the back of my polyester horse-printed shirt, but I might as well have. Because we'd moved so many times, I was shy and quiet. And in my junior high, shyness was as much a social liability as corrective shoes, headgear, or a love of fantasy in a school that seemed to reward the extroverts and popular kids who liked things such as football and cheerleading. I became a passive victim, guzzling a bully-me cocktail: mix together equal parts low self-esteem and social awkwardness with a dash of desperation and stir.

With Lizzie, it's different. We talk about many things that I never did with my parents as a kid. I may have passed my shyness on to Lizzie, like a family heirloom, but she seems to feel more comfortable in her skin than I did as a middle schooler. I know I can't buffer her from every mean girl and from every disappointment, as much as I'd love to do so, but I've found that discussing my own experience with her about how I was seems to help keep the dialogue going. Letting her know that adults have been there seems to help take some invisible weight off her, lightening the pain of being left out. When I told her I contacted Jane, she seemed surprised. "The bus bully?" she asked. I relayed our conversation, mentioning why Jane thought she'd been a bully.

"So that's why she was so mean? It didn't sound like she was very happy," Lizzie said.

I told Lizzie I suspected she was right and that I sincerely wished I'd said something to Jane a long time ago, that I'd been brave enough to turn around in that bus seat and ask her, "Why are you being mean?" Lizzie nodded.

Jane now has a fifteen-year-old daughter, so she is extremely cognizant of bullying and its effects. "I'm working very hard at teaching her to not be critical and to be accepting of others who are different, but she gets frustrated with me." In fact, she later shared our conversation with her daughter, admitting to her own daughter that she'd been a mean girl all those years ago. She wrote that the revelation left her daughter speechless.

And just like that, more than three decades after Jane had made me cry, she did it again.

"YOU AND DAD DO THAT?"

M y daughter crawled into the car and snapped her seat belt shut, even more excited than usual after a recent party.

"We talked about boys," Lizzie said, giggling like a schoolgirl. Which, at twelve, is exactly what she is.

It seems like just a few weeks ago Lizzie thought boys were icky. Because fourteen days earlier, to be exact, they were: I'd taken her to a movie where, during a scene when the main characters kissed, she'd covered her eyes and squealed, "Ewww!"

As my husband and I listened to Lizzie chatter excitedly about what she considered her ideal qualities in a boy ("kind and smart, with red hair, tanned skin, and enchanting green eyes"), we exchanged a glance. I needed to figure out what to say during our next "talk"—and I needed to do it soon. I'd been discussing her body and sexuality with Lizzie for as long as she could speak—since before, actually. I used proper terms for genitals when I changed her diaper as an infant, read her age-appropriate books about reproduction (with talking cartoon sperm!) when she was younger, and gave her more-detailed ones as puberty neared. The lessons seemed to take. As a toddler, she helpfully informed a play group buddy that "I have a 'gina 'cause I a girl—you have a penis 'cause you not." But those earlier conversations now seemed so abstract and easy—sexuality isn't sex.

The thought of talking to my daughter about sex—and that one day in the distant future she might actually have it—scares me in a whole new way. Now that she's beginning to get interested in boys, we've got to discuss not just cartoon sperm, but what can happen when the real ones meet a 'gina—with any and all possible outcomes. Those earlier talks didn't have anything to do with our daughter liking boys. Or even "like-liking" them.

"If you like-like a boy, you talk about him with your friends at sleepovers, and if you're really brave, you can even tell him," she answered when I inquired after the party where they'd discussed boys what it meant to like-like someone. She added, "But we wouldn't do anything romantic, like in the olden days."

I suspect Lizzie viewed "the olden days" as a time where gentleman callers in top hats, monocles, and gold-tipped walking sticks wooed hoopskirt-wearing young ladies by taking them on jaunts in their horse-drawn carriages.

I thought back to my olden days. Those few years from awkward twelve-year-old to sexually active sixteen-year-old passed so quickly—it was like both a lifetime and minutes. Then, I would never have chatted happily with my parents about boys, ideal qualities or not. Or sexuality. I didn't know what my female parts were called. They were just the anatomically ambiguous but geographically accurate "down there." I quickly careened from seventh-grade crushes so hush-hush that I hardly admitted them to myself to, a few years later, swilling Southern Comfort and having sex with my juvenile delinquent boyfriend in his ancient, primer-spackled Audi. He was an actual delinquent—with a real criminal record, thanks to an unauthorized excursion he'd taken in someone else's vehicle. He seemed exotic and a tad dangerous, as if he belonged in a Technicolor movie version of life, rather than in our seemingly black-and-white small southern town (I mean that literally as well as figuratively—it was both racially divided and very much either-or/good-bad). Our community was also smack dab in the Bible Belt, which felt more each day like a noose tightening around my neck. On the bright side, this relationship helped me get over my bad-boy complex early.

Back then, I'd never had "the talk" with my mom. It would have involved talking, something we didn't do much of. And it would have implied that I had—or was thinking of having—actual sex. So when actual sex led to an actual pregnancy at sixteen, I spent a few panicked days trying to figure out how to tell my parents about what the home pregnancy test confirmed. Having learned firsthand what can happen if there's not honest communication about sex and its consequences, I know how important talking with my daughter can be. But it's scary. Then again, what could happen if we don't speak frightens me even more.

✳ ✳ ✳

Lizzie and I are close. We discuss pretty much everything now. ("Talking to you about boys is awkward, Mom, but seeing you try on a sports bra is disturbing.") I hold no illusions, though: I realize the iron gate of adolescence will come slamming down sometime soon. Twelve is a transitional age: still a girl, but on the cusp of all-out rebellion. Lizzie holds my hand as we walk the dog one minute and pushes it away the next. She hugs me for no reason one morning and storms into her room in an angry huff a few hours later. I'm about as comfortable as Lizzie is with some of the topics I know it's my job as a parent to bring up, but I know I'm going to have to step out of my comfort zone a lot during the next few years. Talking about safe sex and birth control may make us both feel awkward and uncomfortable, but they are issues as tightly woven as the taffeta I wore to my senior prom. I have to discuss them with Lizzie since she will be making choices in the coming years that could, in a matter of minutes, change her life forever.

And I've started: Just the other night, we cuddled together in bed, reading a new sex ed book, *It's Perfectly Normal*, which I'd run out and bought right after the party where my daughter discussed boys. Yes, we were both embarrassed by the dozens of pictures of vulvas and penises and the frank but honest description of sex and its possible consequences, but I soldiered on even as I heard my voice quivering. I think Lizzie could tell I was nervous; she scooted a little closer to me. I want to make sure she's got all the accurate information she needs now so she'll be able to make good choices later. I was glad I had the book, not only to mask my unease, but also to have something to stare at during some of Lizzie's observations. Otherwise, I might have burst out laughing. Talking about sex with Lizzie turned out to be pretty entertaining.

"I'm glad I'm going to get a period instead of that," she said, studying an illustration of a boy waking up from a nocturnal emission.

"When I'm old, I'm definitely going to use birth control, because I don't want a baby every time I have sex." I made sure we read that chapter again. And prayed that by "old," she meant "after college."

We came to a picture of a couple under a blanket. "You and Jeff don't do that, do you?" Lizzie said, pointing. I assured her we did. "I'm never going into your bedroom again!" She actually shuddered. I grinned, relieved I didn't have to worry about Lizzie having sex anytime soon—or about her rummaging through my bedside table.

"Damn it."

"Did she just say what I think she did?"

A crash came from the kitchen, where Lizzie was preparing a "kid dinner," the early meal she enjoys preparing on weekends. A plate on the counter held a chicken tamale, a spinach salad, and a pile of health food cheese puffs. A coffee mug, which had been sitting next to her food, was now on the floor, still in one piece but empty of milk.

"Damn," Lizzie muttered.

I smiled. Four-letter words don't really bother me.

* * *

Back when Lizzie was in third grade, we flew to visit my parents in Arizona during her school's winter break. One crisp morning, we went for a hike on a desert mountain trail to look for ancient petroglyphs. As we sat on reddish rocks to rest, gazing over the saguaro cacti and mesquite, my mom handed Lizzie a snack. Lizzie took some gorp, the hiker's snack of fruit, nuts, and, most important, chocolate, out of a zippered plastic bag and popped a handful in her mouth. An M&M tumbled onto the dusty trail.

"Damn it." Lizzie uttered under her breath.

After the shock subsided from hearing my towheaded child curse for the first time, I felt oddly proud—she'd used the word appropriately. My mom looked at me. I looked at her. We looked at Lizzie. Lizzie looked down at the bag of gorp and dug out another M&M and shoved it in her mouth. I didn't say a thing.

After snack break, as Lizzie took her grandfather's hand and led him up the trail, I hung back with my mom.

"Did she say what I think she did?" I asked my mom.

"It sure sounded like it," she answered.

"School has certainly expanded her vocabulary."

The bus Lizzie took to school also transported several middle school boys who, according to Lizzie's friend's mom, frequently quizzed one another with "four-letter-word spelling tests."

It turns out I never had to say anything to Lizzie that winter since I didn't hear any additional expletives, except for the Movie Incident.

*　*　*

Lizzie and her friend Kate watched *Ghostbusters* during a sleepover. After it was over, they cleared their snack bowls, bringing them into the kitchen.

"That was so good!" Lizzie exclaimed. "But there was lots of swearing."

"They kept saying the C-word," Kate said to me, giggling.

"Uh, really?" I asked, wondering what I was going to say to Kate's mom.

"Yeah, they kept saying"—Lizzie lowered her voice to a whisper—"crap."

Lizzie and Kate snickered.

I was relieved it wasn't the *other* C-word.

* * *

I didn't hear Lizzie curse again until seventh grade, when John Steinbeck made her swear.

In English class that year, they read *The Grapes of Wrath* and kept a journal written from the point of view of one of the characters. My rule-loving daughter chose the foul-mouthed grandfather. Lizzie took to the assignment with gusto, jotting long entries into her journal:

> *A Car Miracle: Wow, today has been a goddamn day. We started to go in our car an' we were rumblin' along when we heard a loud crash. Loud as hell was the sound. It was terrible music to our ears, our car was breakin' down. With a final shriek, the car stop'd. We were stranded. So I snuck off to an old car place while the kids and Martha waited. I went there and by Christ there was a box o' tools on the ground. It were a miracle. I took them back an' fixed her up'. By that time the Warlings and us started up camp again'. Then a man who was ragged indeed came up, asked if we're gonna go to California. He said it was damn awful. I wasn't surprised at all. But heck, Martha and the kids were. We have to go to California because we have no place to go. I'm runn'n out of cigars, soon I will just have my pipe to smoke. Moving to California wouldn't be so bad if they grew cigars on the vines instead of goddamn grapes. Bye.*

In study hall, she enlisted friends to help her edit, which involved reading the journal out loud, over and over.

Since Steinbeck opened the floodgates, she hasn't been able to fully shut them. Jeff and I occasionally hear her mutter the word (right now, "damn" is her only curse word) when she stubs her toe or drops a bag of recycling on the kitchen floor.

We've told her we really don't care if she curses when she's at home, but she needs to remember that some people might look at her funny if she peppers her speech with salty language and that it's often considered disrespectful, especially at places like school or work. She gets it, although she still tests the waters in study hall, if it's part of an assignment. I don't think she'll complain to her math teacher about the damn algebra homework.

On a recent drive to the Columbia River Gorge for a family hike, Lizzie lost her place in the book she'd brought for the hour-and-a-half car trip.

"Damn," we heard, quietly but clearly, from the backseat.

"Damn! Damn!" said Jeff, who was driving. "Look at the damn river."

I joined in the chorus: "It's damn gorgeous! Damn Columbia River Gorge-ous! Damn mountains!"

"Damn car!" Lizzie shouted.

The three of us cursed nonstop—for about a minute. Then Lizzie begged us to quit.

"I don't like how it sounds," she said.

So we stopped.

I still hear the occasional, "Ouch, damn!" but she seems to keep her profanity in the house. For the most part. Hell yeah.

"WILL WE BE AN OFFICIAL FAMILY?"

want to get Jeff something special for his birthday," Lizzie said, rummaging through a shelf packed with new and used books about fish at our local bookstore. Near the end of Lizzie's seventh-grade year, her dad had become interested in saltwater aquariums, and she thought a book about the subject would make the perfect gift. It was a thoughtful idea. I told Lizzie so and that I knew Jeff would love that or anything she decided to get or make for him.

Jeff isn't Lizzie's biological father, but he's her dad. He came into her life after she turned four, and a year later, he became an even bigger part of it when the three of us moved into a small house together. Ten months after that, Jeff and I decided to get married. One big reason we decided to make it legal was Lizzie.

* * *

That Saturday afternoon at our home in upstate New York, I stood in my ivory silk wedding dress, clutching a bouquet, and glanced down at Lizzie, who was then six and still went by Elizabeth. She was standing frozen next to me, dressed in a satiny gown and sneakers, holding a basket filled with rose petals.

"Now will we be an official family?" she asked, looking up at me.

Squeezing her hand, I assured her we would.

I gazed at Jeff. He smiled. Our family was finally about to become an "official" one.

Not many years before that, I assumed my family would be a traditional one, which was odd since I've never been a conventional person. I met the man who'd become my first husband in college, and we were together for eighteen years. Eschewing the typical postcollege path of an entry-level job and power suits with shoulder pads (it was the eighties), I set out with Mike on another route, traveling the world while cobbling together whatever jobs we could.

We finally settled down in New York City and got married. I believed that we'd live happily ever after, as our parents seemed to after they'd married. Both of our sets of parents had met after college and been together since the early 1960s. To us, their relationships appeared as solid as the bedrock our Manhattan tenement was built on. I assumed our lives would be similar. But it didn't turn out that way.

After we'd been together thirteen years, Mike had his first psychotic episode. Psychotic episode. How I hate that phrase. It makes mental illness sound like an inane sitcom instead of the nightmare it can be. I spent the final five years of our marriage fruitlessly trying to make him better. I took him to doctors, collecting diagnoses as though they were baseball cards: depression, major depression with psychotic features, bipolar disorder. Each diagnosis seemed a little scarier than the previous one. His doctors told us that bipolar disorder, although not curable, was treatable, like diabetes—as long as Mike took his pills. But he didn't like taking them and often stopped once they started working.

During a prolonged "better" period, we got pregnant. I just knew a baby would help Mike stay well—if he wouldn't take his pills for himself or for me, of course he would for his child. But I was wrong. Eventually I left with our daughter. I'd tried; I spent five years counting his pills, begging him to take them. I made countless excuses to friends—and to myself—for missing their children's birthday parties because Mike had gone off his medicine yet again. I watched him ignore our daughter as she held her arms open wide for a hug. One morning, after a prolonged manic episode during which he had been up for days, I woke to find all the pictures of my family turned over. I finally realized nothing would change unless I did—and that our relationship was over. I gave it my all until I gave up.

So I became a single mom. And as is the case with many single moms of young children, my daughter's social life became mine. Lizzie and I dug in the sandbox with red plastic shovels, jumped into piles of crunchy fall leaves in the park, and went on countless playdates, her friends' mothers my main link to the adult world. But after a year, it felt as if something were missing from my life—extended conversations with people over the age of three. I missed adult company. I started dating and soon met the man who'd one day become my second husband.

Jeff and I met online, flirting and getting to know each other remotely. When Jeff and I met in person, very early on we knew we had something real. But when Lizzie and Jeff finally met, we knew—deep inside before we'd even admit it out loud—that we'd found a family. As time passed and our relationship deepened, it all seemed easy and natural. I'd tried for so long to make my marriage work by myself that I'd never realized how exhausting it was until it was over. Because Mike had been so sick, even when we were together I was practically a single parent to Lizzie. Diapers, feeding, bathing—all fell to me. Being in a healthy relationship with a rational man felt . . . good. This was a new and unusual sensation. At first I was certain something was wrong, that I was missing a slew of wildly fluttering red flags. But I relaxed and trusted my gut. Jeff actually wanted to parent—he checked out a stack of parenting books from the library, and late at night, while Lizzie slept under her favorite red "kitty comforter," we discussed them. Although we tried to take things slow for Lizzie's sake, it was as if we'd been thrown into a perpetual motion machine—and our relationship kept moving ahead on its own, and a little over a year after we met, we moved in together.

Lizzie finally had an unswerving relationship with a "dad." He was not her biological father, but he was there, both physically and emotionally, each and every day for her. And as they grew closer, there was never any question that he had become the father she'd never really had. Sometimes I'd stand near the doorway to Lizzie's room, tucked around the corner out of sight, and listen as Lizzie demanded to hear her favorite story again, one that Jeff had invented. Jeff would sigh theatrically and say, "Okay—but this is the last time." And then, lowering his voice, he'd begin:

Once upon a time, I didn't have a family. I was sad because I really wanted one, so I searched the world, looking. I went to the post office and asked if they had any families. 'Just stamps,' the mailman said. So I left, sad. I went to the pizzeria to get a cheese slice. I asked if they had any families. 'No families, just pizza,' the pizza woman said. So I ordered a slice and ate it unhappily. I went to the grocery store and asked if they had a family. 'We had one last week, but we're fresh out. We do have lovely red apples, though,' the grocer said. So I glumly bought some. On the way home, the apples tumbled out of the bag and I started to cry. A nice woman stopped and helped me pick them up. Her little blond daughter asked why I was crying. I told her I didn't have a family. She said if her mom said it was okay, I could be part of theirs. It was. And that's how I found my family.

"Again!" Lizzie would squeal. I smiled from the doorway of Lizzie's room as I watched her nestle into the crook of Jeff's arm and giggle. And Jeff told the story again.

Over the years, Mike's contact with Lizzie has been infrequent. Months and, occasionally, years go by without hearing from Mike at all. Then he'll call, casually, as if he just saw her that morning, saying, "Lizzie, it's Dad." The conversation always seems slightly off-kilter. She knows Mike's sickness makes him act the way he does and that any emotion she experiences is okay. During previous visits, she's clung to my hand and lingered near me. Lizzie is polite with Mike in the same way she is with a stranger, making small talk and sitting up straight. Shortly before we separated, one night when I tucked her in, she whispered, "I don't like Daddy really much." Mostly, though, Lizzie doesn't mention him and becomes visibly uncomfortable when he phones, stiffening in her chair as she clutches the phone. But I'm not sure how much she really understands and what she really thinks. Out of necessity, we listen in on conversations. He'll ask, many times in a row, if she wants a guitar. When she politely says, "No, thank you," and that she really likes playing the piano and saxophone, he ignores her and tells her she really should play guitar. She can join a band!

When Mike is not taking his medication, it's far worse: she might get a series of packages from him. Experience has taught us to intercept manila envelopes plastered with dozens and dozens of stamps, filled with broken CDs and essays about his drunken exploits. At times, he has written that she should go to church (she doesn't) and warned her against Jeff, because he is Jewish. He's sent her notes questioning his paternity. He occasionally includes a grab bag of items he clearly has around his apartment: a portable radio, a broken plastic watch, magazines that aren't for children. We give her what we can and store the rest away. She sees him maybe once a year, on visits arranged by his mother.

* * *

Jeff and I talk about almost everything. Lizzie is, and has always been, part of the conversation. Unlike her biological father, Jeff's seen and helped Lizzie grow, from a preschooler who skipped to the playground often wearing a tulle skirt and a tiara to a thirteen-year-old who loves to read fantasy, is writing her own novel, and is starting to think about college and boys. Jeff knows the minutiae of her life. He knows the names of her friends, including that of her very first crush. He can sense, without a word from her, if it's been a bad day in middle school.

When Lizzie was in sixth grade, Mike and his mom visited us in Portland and we invited them to our house for dinner. Mike left the table many times to go outside and smoke. Lizzie, although polite to him, hovered near Jeff and was quiet for much of the meal. After dinner, we drove

Mike and his mom to their hotel, and on the way home, we talked. Jeff asked, "So, sweetie, how did it feel to see Mike?"

"Okay, but odd," Lizzie said.

"What do you mean?" he inquired, voice neutral.

Lizzie paused for a minute, lost in thought, and replied, "Think of my life as a box. My friends and loving family are in the box and Mike is outside it."

Jeff and I exchanged a glance, trying hard but without much success to hold back the tears. Sometimes it was hard to read Lizzie, to know what she was thinking about Mike. But she obviously had been sorting through her feelings on her own. I reached over and rubbed Jeff's shoulder, then twisted in my seat to grab Lizzie's hand, so grateful for our "official" family.

✳ ✳ ✳

The night of Jeff's birthday, after we'd eaten large slices of angel food cake, Lizzie darted out of the dining room and returned carrying a couple of gifts wrapped in holiday paper. As Jeff unwrapped a book about saltwater fish, he looked over at Lizzie.

"It's perfect!" he said.

She beamed.

"WHAT IF I DON'T MAKE ANY FRIENDS?"

When my daughter, Elizabeth, was five, our family fled New York City in search of the perfect place to raise kids. A small town in the Hudson Valley surrounded by organic farms and filled with other families with young children seemed wholesome and idyllic. Elizabeth had forty acres behind our small house to roam and a climbing structure that, over the six years we lived there, transformed into whatever her imagination desired:

"Want to sail on my pirate ship, Mommy?" she asked at five, red silk sash tied around her waist.

"It is I, Princess Elizabeth! Welcome to my castle!" she announced at seven as she took off her silver crown and waved it benevolently at her kingdom's sole subject.

"Mom, can Kate and I have more cookies in our clubhouse?" she requested at ten, grabbing the box before I could give an answer.

We plucked tart apples from low-hanging branches and picked giant sunflowers that were almost bigger than her. In summer, she hiked in the nature preserve and splashed in swimming holes. In winter, she sledded on the small hill behind the elementary school.

Elizabeth seemed to love it there, but I didn't. Although I adored parts of it, country life wasn't for me. Something was missing—there was a hole in the whole. I bought muck boots and flannel-lined jeans, attempting to channel the rural person I thought might be tucked away inside. But she stayed hidden. Meanwhile, I craved the energy of the city I'd left behind. New York City had been infinite possibility, condensed. The countryside just seemed like infinite space. Although my husband, Jeff, loved the town's quiet, he felt far removed from urban life as well. On one of our date nights, after a forty-minute drive from our house to our favorite artsy theater, we sat down to veggie burgers at a bistro before the show. Jeff took a sip of iced tea and looked over at me.

"I feel like we're so far from everything. It makes me feel really out of the loop," he said.

I knew exactly what he meant.

*　*　*

Over the six years we lived there, it sometimes seemed a little as if I were doing time—that I was locked in a four-wheel prison, constantly driving between playdates, work, and school. As Elizabeth grew older, the number of miles I drove seemed to grow, too. Although all that driving could be merely inconvenient, it became downright terrifying in the winter when it snowed. Which it did—a lot. During one such winter day, while Elizabeth (then ten), Jeff, and I shoveled the driveway for the fifth time in three days after yet another snowstorm, we decided to move.

"You know, I can't believe I used to like snow," Elizabeth said, wrestling with her shovel.

We thought about moving back to New York City, but the idea of squeezing our lives back into an eight-hundred-square-foot apartment felt claustrophobic after country life. New York was a chapter closed, and our love affair with it had long ended. We wanted the excitement of a new relationship, so we decided to leave our former love for a younger, hipper one—an outdoorsy one filled with creative types and cheaper housing. Portland, Oregon, had caught our eye during a trip several years earlier.

We had really fallen in love with Portland, with its food carts, its bookstores, and its "do it yourself" vibe. We liked that biking to work and backyard chickens were as common as places to grab an excellent espresso. We originally didn't give relocating there any more thought than we would moving to Vientiane. It was three thousand miles away. Interesting place, yes, but moving to it wasn't practical. We also had no compelling reason to move: no job waiting for us out there and no family. But, Jeff and I pondered, couldn't we take our jobs with us? Since we're both writers and work from home, we could do so remotely and not feel so remote. Then again, our daughter was happy in the Hudson Valley. But should her contentment trump our unhappiness? And how much of her contentment came from not having really experienced life anyplace else? It's easy to be satisfied if you don't know what you're missing.

Yet Portland, the concept, wouldn't leave us alone. During another visit a year or so later, as part of a group reading at Powell's Books, Jeff and I explored both the city and the possibility of living there. We toured some middle schools and visited a real estate agent. We drove around residential neighborhoods in our rental car, envisioning which might become ours, taking flyers from boxes in front of all the houses for sale, fantasizing about which room would be ours, which one Elizabeth's. We saw children riding bikes and families strolling on sidewalks together. Everyone looked so happy. I pictured Elizabeth riding her bike to the local pool with new friends instead of having to be driven everywhere. She could be spontaneous instead of needing her playdates planned in advance via e-mail and date books. Somehow during that trip, fantasy became reality, and we knew Portland was meant to be our new home.

I told myself Portland was a much better fit, not only for ex-city folks Jeff and me but for Elizabeth, too. That she'd easily make friends. I assured myself, because her new school started in sixth grade, everyone there was new; no one was going to be singled out as the new kid. That as she got older, she was going to want more independence, and public transportation would give her that. That there was far more for teenagers to do than hang out at the town's movie theater or cruise its one main street. But was I trying to talk myself into believing this? Could I be in denial that Jeff and I were selfishly choosing what we wanted over what might be better for her? Deep inside, I knew our move was the right thing to do.

To make sure it felt right to all of us, I took Elizabeth on a mother/daughter visit to Portland for a week. It was part reconnaissance mission, part PR blitz. We got treats at Voodoo Doughnut. Elizabeth chose the jam-filled one shaped like a person and bit off its "arm."

"The 'blood' is delicious!" she cried, laughing as she licked some raspberry jelly from her fingers.

We visited a couple of schools.

"People here are really nice," she said. She seemed somewhat surprised, as if this were a quality found only in New York.

We spent a few hours at the giant bookstore, Powell's.

"Wow," Elizabeth said, her eyes widening in wonder. "This is even better than the bookstores back home."

* * *

Once we knew Elizabeth was on board, too, we had to sell our home. We put our house on the market, accepted an offer, and Elizabeth started her farewell tour.

"We'll write to each other and we can even video chat," she said to her friend Kate at one of many "good-bye" sleepovers. She added, "And I'm coming back to New York every summer so we'll see each other!"

A few weeks before Elizabeth started sixth grade, we watched as most of what we owned was carted onto an eighteen-wheeler.

"Bye, room. I'll miss you," she said softly as we walked through our house one final time before we left. Her voice echoed in its emptiness.

Then we loaded our silver Prius with a suitcase, our kid, and our dog and began a 3,439-mile road trip. Elizabeth flipped open her notebook and jotted a poem about the move. One line of it read: "Remember when my friend and I jumped on this empty space that once was my bed?" She snapped her notebook shut and opened her map, tracing the route with her finger. Excited about the trip, she'd researched what she wanted to see and where she wanted to go. But she worried, too.

"What if I can't get a library card?" she asked somewhere in Pennsylvania.

"What if kids think I'm weird?" she wanted to know in Sioux Falls, South Dakota.

"What if I don't make any friends?" she worried outside Bozeman, Montana.

I tried to answer her questions.

"I know for a fact you'll be able to get a library card. We can do that before school starts," I replied, twisting in the front seat to look at her in Pennsylvania.

"Hey, being weird is a good thing in this family," I said in South Dakota. (It was true.)

"I know it's hard, but you'll make friends," I assured her in Montana.

I looked back at Elizabeth. She was staring out the window.

* * *

But her questions had raised my own, which I kept silent. What if she didn't make friends? Like a post-traumatic stress survivor, I had flashbacks to my first day of seventh grade, a new kid just moved to Slidell, Louisiana. My dad, who worked as a geophysicist for an oil company, had been transferred to Jakarta, Indonesia, before I started fourth grade. We had just spent three glorious years there, which was the longest I'd ever lived in one place. Moving back to the States, to a small town, wasn't just a culture shock, it was a total shock. In a time and place where most of the other twelve-year-olds were wearing jeans with thin gold belts, blue eye shadow, and feathered hair, I was decked out for the first day of school in a batik wraparound skirt and a clashing PROPERTY OF THE MACADAMIA NUT FACTORY T-shirt. It did not go well.

Thinking about my own first day of middle school as we passed seemingly endless fields of genetically modified corn,

I wondered if we should have stayed in the Hudson Valley. Or would we have been better off moving back to a tiny apartment in Brooklyn, where Elizabeth still had friends? I shook it off, reminding myself that even though junior high got off to a bumpy start, I did eventually make friends—and I was certain Elizabeth would, too. I vowed to help edit her clothing selection for the first day of school.

*　*　*

Every family should take a cross-country trip once. Because once is probably enough. We hit the sights Elizabeth had wanted to see—the "Big Heads" of Mount Rushmore, the Corn Palace, and a water park. We saw the places Jeff and I wanted to see: the Badlands and an 1880s ghost town filled with dilapidated robots. We stopped where Louis the Dog, our corgi–Australian shepherd mix, wanted—random parking lots and fire hydrants. Nine days, twelve states, and many cups of coffee later, we pulled into the driveway of our new home, a 1927 bungalow. We climbed up wooden steps and sat on the porch swing, rocking gently, waiting to meet our real estate agent to collect the keys. Two women walked toward us from their homes across the street, smiling, and introduced themselves. "My daughter is so excited another sixth grader is moving in. What's your name?" one of them asked my daughter.

"Eliz . . . I mean Lizzie." And Lizzie smiled.

My daughter had left New York as Elizabeth and, three thousand miles later, had become Lizzie.

A few moments later, after the real estate agent dropped off the keys and Lizzie had chosen her bedroom and the dog rolled around on the lawn, Lizzie spotted the girl across the street and raced outside to introduce herself.

It all seemed so easy that I kept waiting for something bad to happen: the kid across the street to morph into a bully, the moving company to lose all our belongings in Montana, the realization that we'd made a terrible mistake to thwack me in the head. But nothing happened. Instead, each day Portland felt a little more like home. A few days after we'd moved in, I drove a visibly nervous Lizzie to her new school. Would the shyness and social awkwardness that I'd passed on to her like a faulty chromosome make her first day of school a miserable one? I asked her if she wanted me to walk her in.

"No, Mom, I'm fine," she said, then hopped out of the car and darted into her new school building. I smiled and held the steering wheel tightly. That afternoon, she hugged a new friend good-bye.

The second day of school, she wore my old batik wrap-around skirt with leggings.

"ANNA'S BROTHER GOT HIS LEARNER'S PERMIT."

Anna's brother got his learner's permit. He's learning to *drive*!" Lizzie said, emphasizing the last word as we headed over the Hawthorne Bridge and home from school one afternoon. Driving, apparently, was something so exciting that it warranted both italics and an exclamation point. And Lizzie, at thirteen, will be eligible for her learner's permit in less than two years. It seems like just the other day that she was zipping down our road on her shiny purple bicycle with training wheels.

Not all that long ago, I used to fantasize about our daughter having her license. It would make life so much easier! She could shuttle herself from swim team to home to school to piano! Of course, this daydream was along the lines of training our goldendoodle to trot to the supermarket and fetch a quart of milk.

Now that there's a finite time before Lizzie or her friends actually get their licenses, I'm frightened.

"Allie drives some kids to swim team practice after school," Lizzie said, referring to a high school student on the team. "When I'm in high school, could I maybe carpool with them?"

I gulped down my panic and resisted an urge to yell, "No way!"

Our local paper regularly carries stories about teenagers in car accidents, always reminding us that motor vehicle crashes are the leading cause of death for kids thirteen to nineteen. I think about all the young drivers I see holding their steering wheel in one hand and cell phone in the other, maneuvering four thousand pounds of steel through our neighborhood filled with bike-riding and ball-playing children.

It's not just young drivers who are irresponsible—there are plenty of adults who do exactly the same thing, often while their children are strapped into car seats in the back of their minivans. It is terrifying to imagine our child driving down those very streets while someone is motoring toward her and yammering on a cell phone or reading an e-mail.

At least here in Oregon they don't pass out permits to kids like Halloween candy and wave good-bye. As in many other states now, there are guidelines about when teens can drive and who can be in the car with them. This is quite different from when I was a teenager.

* * *

The day I got my learner's permit, I immediately wanted to get behind a wheel. My dad took me out that day for my very first drive. I crawled into our off-white Dodge Aspen station wagon with its vinyl seats that suctioned to my legs in the southern Louisiana heat, even if the air conditioner was cranked all the way up. Nervously—although I'm certain my dad had to be far more so—I inserted the key in the ignition and turned. With a little difficulty, I jiggled the silver gearshift handle into "D" and pressed gingerly on the gas pedal. The car shuttered to a start. I reflexively hit the brake. (Thank goodness we were wearing seat belts or I might have sent us plummeting through the windshield before we'd gone two feet down the road.)

I drove carefully and oh so slowly through the streets of our subdivision, the aspirationally named Country Club Estates, a maze of cul-de-sacs off a central road, all of which fronted small lots with well-tended brick ranch-style houses. The large plastic steering wheel became extremely slippery—the combination of southern heat and my nerves seemed to transform my body into a rain cloud, sprinkling sweat all over the car's interior. Slowly I maneuvered the car up the single lane of Country Club Boulevard, which was both "country club" and "boulevard" in name only, made the circle at the end of it, and started homeward. I looked over at my dad and smiled, feeling much more confident of my skills. Even Speed Racer had to learn how to drive at some point! This was fun! I relaxed. And hit a mailbox. Thankfully, my dad, the car, and the mailbox were all fine—rather, the mailbox was almost fine. My dad got out of the station wagon to let the home owner know that it looked a little different from the way it had moments before.

Today, my husband gently mocks how I drive, saying I do so like a little old lady, sitting straight up at attention, elbows level, clutching the steering wheel firmly and punctually at ten and two o'clock, while keeping consistently just under the speed limit. I've been an overly cautious driver for a long time. But as a teen, I didn't always drive so carefully.

Back then, once you had a license you owned the road. The road being the town's main drag, Gause Boulevard. In our small town, there wasn't much for high school kids to do on weekends except "cruise Gause." The proper way to do this was by loading up the car with a bunch of friends and driving up and down the road after procuring beer with the help of someone a few years older. (The legal drinking age then was eighteen.) We turned up the music to "deaf by thirty" and shouted at one another, checking out the other cars and big trucks. I remember turning around, as I drove, to better hear a friend in the backseat. Distractions, teenage drivers, and beer—not the safest combination. And if we tired of this (which we quickly did), a resourceful sixteen-year-old found it pretty easy to sneak into bars with a fake ID. And our town was filled with resourceful youth. Driver's licenses then were often just a piece of paper without a photo, easy to make for anyone with access to a typewriter, Wite-Out, and the photocopy machine and laminator at the local drugstore. The trick to a decent fake ID was to use your real first name coupled with a fake surname and a birthday that put you closer to eighteen than, say, twenty-eight.

Teen drinking and driving seemed to go together as naturally as rum and Coke. Everyone I knew who had a vehicle drank. How could they not? The local bars offered their customers (even underage ones) plastic "go cups" so they could take their drinks out to their cars. There were liquor stores all over town (including one with a pull-in bay, like an auto repair shop, where a driver could pull up and load up). Our town also had a drive-through frozen daiquiri shop, one that served iced sugary treats in a rainbow of colors. And in a town where there were mixed messages about drinking and driving everywhere, as a teen I did both.

It took a little while, but the horror stories eventually started to collect and multiply. My first year of college, I heard that a boy a few years ahead of me in high school had died in a drunk driving accident. His van had hit a tree and rolled over. I knew that van. My boyfriend and I had smoked pot in the back of it a few years earlier. There were other accidents, other hospitalizations, other deaths. The stupidity of what I'd done sank in.

Thankfully, I never killed anyone—myself included—and never got into an accident while drinking, but it was pure luck that I didn't drive off a bridge into a bayou or into a cluster of pedestrians.

* * *

When Lizzie gets her permit and eventually her license, she'll face not only the possibilities of driving drunk or encountering other drunk drivers, but also distractions that we never imagined: cell phones and iPods and even the GPS.

Lizzie never sees me talk on the phone and drive—I don't. I have my radio buttons preset or I listen to whatever is already in the CD player. She sees me tap addresses into the GPS while we're in our driveway or I ask her to do so if we're driving. Will these habits transfer to her by some sort of good-example osmosis? I hope so. She's a responsible kid, and I think she'll continue to be so. We discuss safe driving habits now, a few years before she'll actually get behind a wheel; I give hypothetical examples of what might happen and let her come up with possible answers.

"What if you're on a date with a really cute boy you have a major crush on, and he wants to have a beer?" I asked.

"I'd just say, 'I'll drive if you want to drink,'" she said.

"Or you're with friends at a party and the driver has had a drink or two?" Jeff added.

"Hmmm. I'd volunteer to drive."

"What if he or she said no, thanks, that they were okay?" Lizzie tapped her fingers on the table as she thought.

"I'd call you from the party so you could pick me up."

"What if it's midnight?" I asked.

"Would it be okay to call that late?" Lizzie asked tentatively. She knows we go to sleep early.

"Of course. We'd much rather have you call us than ride in a car with someone who's been drinking," Jeff said, adding, "no matter what time it is."

"What if you're driving and your phone rings and you've been expecting a really important call?" I ask.

"I'd either let it go to voice mail or pull over and park," Lizzie said, certain of this answer.

But there's no peer pressure in our dining room. And outside our house, in the real world, she may indeed answer questions like these quite differently. What will she really do if she crawls into a car stuffed with other teens and the driver swivels her head to gossip? What if she's on a date and is offered a beer by someone she's infatuated with? Will she have the courage to say that she doesn't want to be in a car with someone distracted or drinking and that she'd like to get out of the car and call her parents? I certainly didn't have the confidence to do that. Will she say something or will she go along with the crowd, blindly believing that nothing can go wrong? Like most teenagers, Lizzie wants to fit in.

When I look into Lizzie's face, I still see in it the little girl she used to be, who wanted me to check under her bed for monsters each night. I know she's growing up and I can't glance into a crystal ball to foresee the future, so I have to trust that Lizzie will make good choices as a driver and as a passenger. I hope little pieces of our conversations lodge in her head, so she'll keep her phone off or silent, even when I'm not there to tell her to do so, so she's not tempted if it rings.

* ※ *

Driving is yet another huge leap of faith—for us as parents, as well as for Lizzie. She will soon be pulling away, literally, down the driveway and seeing us and her childhood in the rearview mirror. I know that one day in the not too distant future, I'll give her the keys and let go. Or maybe not. Our city does have a fine public transportation system, after all.

"WILL SHE BE OKAY AT CAMP?"

The green backpack Lizzie was stuffing with clothes for summer camp was almost as big as she was. At ten, my daughter would soon be off to sleep-away camp for the first time. As she placed Stripey, her stuffed tiger, on top and snapped the bag shut, there were plenty of emotions swirling around the room: nervousness, agitation, anxiety.

And that was just me.

It was Lizzie's first time away from home. I worried that she wouldn't make friends or that she'd be homesick and cry herself to sleep each night. But two days later, driving through Vermont's lush green hills dotted with dairy farms on the way to camp, Lizzie was her usual chattering self.

"What if I fail the swimming test?" Lizzie fretted. She was apprehensive about the upcoming swimming test she'd read about in the camp's welcome letter, worried that she wouldn't be able to tread water for the required time. But she was excited to get there, unpack, and meet new friends.

After Jeff and I helped lug her backpack and duffel bag up the hill to her cabin, we strung mosquito netting over her

55

top pine bunk in an intricate cat's cradle of cord while she dug out her swimsuit. As we sweated and grimaced, Lizzie introduced herself to a new friend and they trotted off to the bathroom to change. They skipped together to the lake for their swimming tests, leaving two sets of nervous parents trying to finish mosquito-proofing their children's bunks. When the girls returned, jabbering to each other nonstop, it was almost as if we'd turned invisible. Jeff and I kissed Lizzie good-bye and left. I was relieved she seemed so happy.

For the first time, we began to think about life with just the two of us, rather than a family of three—what would we do for the next two weeks? It was our first-ever extended alone time, and the possibilities seemed endless. Jeff started the car, and as we bumped along the gravel road away from camp, I was elated—sending her to camp was the right thing to do. Jeff reached over, rubbed my back, and smiled.

Later that night, when I walked by Lizzie's room, I got an uncomfortable feeling that some part of our life was missing—like a phantom limb, an entity that should be there wasn't. I peered in, almost expecting to see her sprawled under her comforter, her dog curled into a crescent at her feet. But her bed was empty. Even her dog avoided the room, as if staying in Lizzie's room without her were as wrong as jumping onto the sofa.

The next evening, Lizzie haunted our dinner date, too. Instead of gazing dreamily into each other's eyes, we took turns guessing what she might be doing at that very moment. And our conjecture transformed into my worry. Had she made any friends? Was she homesick? I had flashbacks to my adolescence, and my mind swarmed with the faces of girls who'd taunted me and made me feel like crawling into myself. Jeff assured me that I was fretting for nothing—that

I was probably just transferring my issues onto Lizzie and it was better left to a discussion with my therapist than making myself nuts over my daughter's imaginary tormentors. He reminded me of how she was when we'd left her at camp—ecstatic with a new friend. Surely not that much had changed in twenty-four hours.

* * *

After a few days, we settled into our new, child-free routine and started to enjoy ourselves—until we received our first postcard. In careful squiggles on a prestamped postcard, Lizzie wrote: "I'm having fun. I'm doing distance swimming. I've had no mail. Please send letters." A picture of a sad face was etched next to the map she'd drawn of the lake and her distance swimming route. A week before she left, I'd posted two letters so she'd have a couple of notes from home waiting for her. They probably just hadn't arrived yet.

A few days later, we stopped at the mailbox late at night, returning from a date in the city. Flipping through the catalogs and bills, we found another postcard: "I like camp. Please send mail. I'm the only person who didn't get any mail." Next to the note was a picture of a blank piece of paper, a pencil, and a stamp. Underneath was a caption: "0 mail." I started to panic. Where was her mail? Was something insidious going on? A plot to keep mail from her? A mean girl in charge of mail duty, purposefully hiding letters from our daughter? A bomb had obliterated the quaint Vermont post office? I was obviously losing my mind. But she should have received at least a few letters by then. Her dad and I had mailed four or five. Her grandparents had sent mail, and a friend had mailed her a postcard. Why had she received "0 mail"? It was too late to call the camp, so I shot off a quick e-mail to the camp administrator, crawled into bed, and slept fitfully. Early the next morning, the camp director called. It was Saturday and the office was closed, but she said she'd checked with Lizzie's counselor, who said our daughter was happy. The director said she would contact the office Monday morning when it opened to see what had happened to Lizzie's mail.

The missing letters enveloped me in helplessness, and despite the director's reassurances, I couldn't stop worrying that Lizzie was miserable at camp. I'm not usually a neurotic, overprotective parent. Sure, when Lizzie was a newborn I made my parents scrub their hands before they held her, but by the time she was thirteen months old I was picking up the Goldfish crackers she'd dropped in the sandbox, dusting them off, and handing them back to her to pop in her mouth. At three, she skipped happily off to preschool—and I spied on her through the classroom window for only the first few days. She was pretty well-adjusted, and I liked to think that I was, too. But somehow the missing letters had turned me into Crazy Mom, envisioning anything—and everything—that might possibly go wrong.

Finally, Monday arrived. The post office was open. The camp director called and said she'd talked to Lizzie. She had finally received the mail and, most important, had been having a blast all along. Somehow her cards to us had been written before the camp's post office had sorted and delivered the ones we'd sent her, and even though I had assumed this might have been the case, her second postcard had sent me into a wild panic. When I heard she'd been enjoying herself the entire time, I realized even though we had sent Lizzie to camp to learn about herself and grow, I was the one who needed to learn—about letting go. Subconsciously, I was still longing for the tiny baby who depended on me for all her needs, but my daughter was growing up. And sooner rather than later, she was going to have a life without me.

I exhaled relief, and Jeff and I enjoyed our last week alone.

When the final day of camp arrived, we drove up, parked the car, and hiked up the hill to Lizzie's cabin. She actually looked taller, more poised, more sure of herself. "May I show you around my camp?" she asked, and without waiting for our answer, she took our hands to show us around, then begged, "Can I come back next year—please?"

And she did go back the following year—and every summer since. A few days ago, we took her backpack and duffel bag out of the living room closet and we've been packing, stuffing them with her canteen and spork, her sleeping bag and mosquito netting. This summer will be her fifth visit to camp. She's never had a mail mix-up since. And I'm finally learning to relax and let go—a little bit, anyway.

"I'M ANGRY AT YOU!"

I lugged the laundry basket filled with freshly washed and haphazardly folded clothes into Lizzie's room and dropped it on her aqua shag rug. Lizzie was sprawled on her bed, absorbed in a book. A mountain of clean clothes was piled on her desk, where they'd been sitting for the last few days.

"I'd like you to put away all your clothes anytime before dinner. And when you're done, please bring the basket downstairs. I need it," I said. Lizzie's room, a Bermuda Triangle for laundry baskets, was starting to resemble a rummage sale.

She put down her book and glared at me as though I'd demanded she drown a litter of kittens.

"I'm *angry* at you!" she spit out.

"Sweetie, it's fine to be angry with me. I'm glad you're telling me," I said evenly as I left her room.

❋ ❋ ❋

I'm happy Lizzie feels comfortable telling me she's irritated. Lately, though, these bursts have been occurring more frequently, almost as if they're volcanic rumblings, to prepare me for the temperamental eruptions of an older teen. When Lizzie is furious, most of the time I smile and calmly tell her she's going to be mad at me a lot during the next few years—I'll love her no matter how she feels. Then I ignore the sighs of exasperation and say something like, "That's my job: to annoy you as much as possible. . . .

"I'm getting pretty good at it, huh?" I add.

* * *

Young teens can be emotional vortexes. I try not to get sucked into the drama. Sometimes Lizzie states her sentiments clearly and other times Albert Einstein couldn't figure her out. It would be much easier if she were just expressing the usual teenage anger, but with her it's more complicated. Her biological father and I split when she was three. Jeff came into our lives when she was four. I think a subconscious part of her may still worry about how she fits in to our family— if she gets too angry at me, would I choose Jeff over her? Of course the rational part of her knows this is nonsense, but, like everyone, she's got bits of her past lodged in her psyche. And I'm sure, locked away in some small cells of her temporal lobe, she's got to feel some residual rejection from her biological father disappearing from her life when she was so young. We do talk about these things, but although she denies they're issues for her, I can't help worrying.

Reading Lizzie is like tearing into a book on astrophysics. I may be able read the words on the page, but I have absolutely no idea what they mean. This is when I have to whisk out my supersecret decoder ring so I can decipher what she's *really* saying. What seems on the surface to be normal conversation often has a very different meaning. And at times my words need interpreting, too.

Here's a translation of a recent conversation Lizzie and I recently had one day after school in our dining room. I was sitting at the table, working on my laptop, and Lizzie had just brought in a snack of milk and tandoori naan from the kitchen.

We said . . .	We meant . . .
Mom: *(looks up from computer)* Hi, sweetie. How was your day?	
Lizzie: *(looks down at plate, not smiling, not frowning)* "It was good."	"It was not especially good."
Lizzie: *(takes a bite of Indian bread and chews, staring into distance)*	
Mom: "Oh?"	"I'd love to hear more. I know that you're not telling all."
Lizzie: "Yeah, I didn't do such a great job on my English essay."	"I'm not happy with it and I suspect you will be even less so."
Mom: "As long as you're taking your time and not rushing. Did you understand what you could do differently next time?"	"Will she get into college or will she end up working the counter at McDonald's?"

Mom:	
(hits SAVE on laptop and closes it, deciding to ask about an incident that occurred the previous week)	
"Hey, how was Jill today?"	"Was Jill as mean as she was on Friday? I dislike her very, very much."

Lizzie:	
(takes a slug of milk before answering)	
"She's okay."	"She's a jerk. But I don't want to say that because I'm not mean like she is."

Mom:	
(quiet, trying to decide exactly what to say)	

Lizzie:	
(smiles, eyes sparkling)	
"Lunch was good. I sat with Eleanor today. She's nice."	"Lunch was the best! Eleanor is great!"

Mom:	
(grins)	
"Sounds good!"	"It does sound good. I'm relieved that awful child is no longer a 'friend.' For now."

The word *okay*, though short, is long on meanings that I try to translate based on context and inflection. If Lizzie says something is okay, most of the time I know that it's really not and I don't want to let it stand. I want to call her on it, but in a way that will allow her to save face. So when she says something like "Jill's okay," her father or I might ask: "Is she okay or 'just okay'?" When Lizzie admits someone is "just okay," we know they usually aren't. We keep talking, keep translating her feelings, and let her know that anything she feels is okay and not "just okay."

Recently, Lizzie became furious at me for no reason I could fathom. We'd been sitting on the sofa one rainy Saturday afternoon, each reading a magazine that had arrived in that day's mail about a half hour earlier. She had an issue of *New Moon* and I had one of *New York*. I could feel the atmosphere in the living room suddenly shift, as if a cold front had arrived unexpectedly. Usually there's a chore to trigger a mood—a bathroom to scrub, a dog to walk, rules to uphold.

"I'm angry at you!" she shouted, and marched into her room, slamming her door and leaving me mystified.

Unfortunately, her room has two doors, one of which is connected to my office and which happened to remain ajar. When I went into my office, I peered into her room through the open door. Lizzie was sitting on her bed, fuming, tapping angrily on her iPod's tiny keyboard.

"Sweetie, slamming the door doesn't have quite as dramatic an effect when the other one stays opened," I said evenly. I smiled, determined to lighten the situation. I wanted to give her an out, if she desired one.

Lizzie looked as though she wished I'd be teletransported to Jupiter, and then she appeared to do a quick mental calculation. She tried to force herself to look angry and failed. She laughed. One crisis diverted. Seven more teenage years' worth to go.

* * *

I was an angry kid. When I was a child, we didn't really discuss our feelings. Instead, my anger built up like a pressure cooker, ready to explode. I think there was a real fear to get emotionally honest in my family. Anger was perceived as messy and something that couldn't be controlled. And my dad loved control. My theory is that it goes back to his childhood. My dad was four and lived on an army base in New York when his father was killed in the Netherlands during World War II. His father's death upended his life. His mother became a distant presence, unable to cope with three young children. My father, who was not a difficult child, was sent away to boarding school, in effect to deal with his sense of loss on his own. It's not unexpected, then, that my dad doesn't like surprises. He has spent his entire adult life trying to plan for everything. Dinner menus decided weeks in advance; mealtimes like clockwork. And real emotion expressed honestly? Forget it—because who knew where real emotions and unchecked anger could lead?

By the time my teenage years rolled around, my parents and I hadn't talked, genuinely, probably ever. And I'd built up an emotional Kevlar vest.

I could be, to put it mildly, difficult. I was not a cuddly teen, all rainbows and ribbons, floating around in a cloud of Love's Baby Soft. I was black concert shirts and tight Calvin Klein jeans, moving about in a cloud of marijuana smoke.

"You're a piece of work!" my dad yelled after I'd challenged yet another rule. Ping. His shouts hit the vest and ricocheted right back.

We'd been slowly retreating into our corners for years, and when I finally came out of mine, I came out swinging.

"Fuck you both!" I screamed at my parents.

But what a defiant kid says and what he or she means are two different things. I wish my parents had been able to interpret my angry words for what they were—the words of an adolescent who wanted independence but was frightened by it (and pretty much everything else). Because what a furious teenager wants more than anything is to be understood and to be told, "I'll love you no matter what. I know you're testing limits, and you can try all you want, but if you break our rules, there are consequences."

Even if the parent has to lie and force these words out, even if he or she is really thinking, *Who the hell is this child? I hate her.*

And if the kid says, "Fuck you! I hate you!" she really means, "Yes, I am filled with animosity, but I actually love you even if I don't and can't show it right now. I'm trying to assert my independence, and you're throwing a big wet blanket on my parade." I wish I could time travel and hand my parents a teen/parent phrase book (or, more likely, throw it at them)—so they could translate what I was saying and what I really meant.

* * *

It's no surprise that as an adult, I also have some unresolved anger. I try to deflect it with humor instead of sending it in a lightning bolt of words toward my husband, but I'm not always successful. I sometimes feel the steam building in that old pressure cooker and still have trouble finding the release valve to let some of it escape. I don't want Lizzie to have the same frustrations, so I talk to her about emotions, letting her know it's okay not only to be angry but also to express it. Some family traditions shouldn't be handed down.

"You're not my boss," Lizzie mumbled under her breath.

"Excuse me?" I said. I'd just asked her for perhaps the tenth time to please clean her bathroom, which I feared was beginning to cultivate new plant life. And although I realize I am not my daughter's boss, "mom" trumps employer/employee relationship.

"That's rude. Go. To. Your. Room." I punctuated each word with full stops.

Lizzie is rarely sent to her room. Because we've taken a proactive approach to parenting, positively reinforcing Lizzie's good behavior since she was a toddler, we usually avoid having to "discipline" her. But sometimes reacting is necessary. And I react negatively to an impolite child. Not that being sent to her room is a cruel and unusual punishment. On any given day, Lizzie spends far more time in her room than she does in the rest of the house, reading, listening to music, writing, or just relaxing. It's just that when an authority figure tells her she has to do something that she may not want to do, it makes her feel powerless, as if she's a little kid. But part of my job as a mom is to occasionally tell her what she doesn't want to hear.

"I didn't mean to say that," Lizzie said, immediately contrite.

"I said, 'Go. To. Your. Room,'" I repeated as calmly as I could. Sometimes I need to breathe slowly when Lizzie makes me angry. I lower my voice and am, to her, frighteningly composed. She knows the quieter I get, the more upset I am.

So into her room she went.

* * *

Back when she was little, till she was about seven years old, short time-outs worked wonders for us. Anxious to please and a lover of rules, Lizzie was usually law-abiding. But since she was a young child, she occasionally needed a shot of discipline when she acted out or freaked out about something, like, at four, wailing that there weren't enough teacups for all her stuffed animals. "And Bunny is thirsty!" she screamed, flinging cups and wooden food across the playroom. Then, we might send her into her room.

"Calm your body down," I'd tell her, adding, "I need you to use your 'normal' voice so I can understand your words."

Alternatively, we would put a much loved stuffed toy in "toy jail" for a few minutes.

"Oopsie, I don't like the words you used to speak to me. Bunny is going to toy jail for two minutes," I'd say, if needed.

"No!" she'd shout.

She could see Bunny on the top of the refrigerator, staring down at her with his glass eyes. A few minutes was just long enough to feel like a punishment to her, but not so long that she'd forget why Bunny was there.

Now that Lizzie is in middle school, a new type of insolence bursts from her occasionally. For instance, if I ask her to carry her dirty clothes to the laundry room, she'll say, "Why don't *you* do it?" I then remind her it's her choice if she wants clean clothes or not, which can result in under-the-breath, unintelligible mutterings. I know it's age-appropriate and that she's testing boundaries and asserting her independence, but disrespect is something that Jeff and I will not put up with (which is kind of ironic, since impudence toward authority was how I spent many of my own teen years). We've seen and heard more than a few classmates direct shockingly rude comments at their parents and watched as their parents said or did nothing (at least in public). We want Lizzie to use "normal" words to tell us that she's angry rather than flinging generalized disdain in our direction. So we've traveled back in time and rediscovered the time-out.

* * *

Minutes after our "who's the boss" moment, Lizzie sat in her room stewing for a bit while I sat in my office working on my computer. There was silence in her room while I typed.

My e-mail dinged.

It was a short message: "I'm sorry. Sent from Lizzie's iPod."

I smiled. I knew she was. I waited a few more minutes and sprung her.

"AREN'T FAMILY VALUES A GOOD THING?"

(modern family talk)

"AREN'T FAMILY VALUES A GOOD THING?"

My parents are Tea Party. I'm a liberal. My husband is to the left of your average Communist. Dinners together walk a tightrope of small talk—none of us wanting to veer too far in either direction, frightened we'll go careening into a political abyss. Lizzie is always a safe topic. She's our Switzerland.

But I'm not sure how much longer that will last. At twelve, Lizzie is quickly becoming politically aware.

She's always been well-informed. Not that she had much of a choice. After the 2000 election and before her first birthday, she participated in her first protest. I stuffed her in her bright green baby backpack and headed to Times Square. There, she grinned and drooled as tourists in fanny packs and white tennis shoes yelled mean things at a dozen of us who were demanding that the votes be counted. The following January, George W. Bush was sworn in—thus ensuring that Lizzie's formative years offered ample opportunities for protest. Her favorite was the huge antiwar rally in Central Park when she was three. There were balloons and face painting, and the playground near the park was bigger and more exciting than

73

the ones back in Brooklyn. Riding the train home, she waved her small paper flag like a sword, chanting, "No Twar! No Twar!" Then she yawned and asked for her sippy cup.

I have never had any intentions of indoctrinating my child in my political beliefs. I want her to make up her own mind. But since she's a kid, she mirrors our beliefs, as her friends do their parents'. If I were a neo-Nazi, a Know Nothing, or a Glenn Beck–listening right-winger, she would probably share my views. But I'm a Prius-driving, composting liberal—and therefore so is Lizzie. (Except the driving part—at twelve, she doesn't yet. Thankfully.) It's not as though we sit her down with Karl Marx flash cards or whisper Howard Zinn to her as she sleeps, but we talk a lot at dinner, discussing politics and what's going on not just in our neighborhood or city but also in the world.

"In Modern Conflicts, we talked about all the bad stuff happening in Congo," Lizzie said before taking a swallow of milk and looking at me. "Didn't you have a student from there?"

I told her I had, when I'd taught English as a second language years earlier.

"I want to travel around Africa, but not there. Not right now, anyway."

Somehow our chat hopped the border to Rwanda, which led to talking about a book I'd taken to the hospital when I was going into labor with Lizzie: Philip Gourevitch's *We Wish to Inform You That Tomorrow We Will Be Killed with Our Families*. (Because I'd never given birth before, I'd assumed I'd have time to dig into a good book between contractions. This wasn't the case.)

Which led our conversation to genocide.

"What's genocide?" Lizzie asked. "I think I know, but I want to make sure."

We told her and mentioned the Holocaust as an example.

"I thought so, but I didn't know that was the name of it," Lizzie said.

Jeff, to change the subject a bit and lighten our dinner conversation, added, "Or it's when a government kills all the Jens in a country."

"And if it's all the Sues, is it suicide? Momicide!" Lizzie laughed.

She knew we weren't making light of government-sanctioned mass murder—our discussions, of world events or politics, can veer from serious to silly quickly. We have our own slightly unique way of looking at world and local events.

But is it possible to balance how we view the world with how other people do? How to make sure that Lizzie is aware of the various outlooks out there, political and other?

✳ ✳ ✳

Our family dinners are very different from the ones I grew up with. Back when I was in second grade, we spent the fall session learning about the upcoming presidential election. One night, as I sat at the table, swinging my legs impatiently, I couldn't wait for dinner to end so I could tell my parents my Very Important News from school that day. I was probably dressed in an outfit like a plaid jumper with a bow affixed to my hair—something that would have fit in more in, say, 1964 Omaha than 1972 San Francisco, where we then lived. I'm pretty sure we were the squarest family sitting down to dinner in San Francisco at that time. (Or doing anything in San Francisco at that time. While other kids were singing along to the Rolling Stones' "Brown Sugar," we attended an Up with People concert.)

Back then, we didn't discuss politics at the dinner table—or anywhere else. Our household was more of a dictatorship, with my dad's conservative beliefs reigning supreme. There was no room for dissent and none encouraged. I learned this pretty early on. But my excitement over sharing my news from the school day trumped my seven-year-old knowledge of our family's hierarchy. I had made up my own mind about an election. Our teacher gave us each a copy of the latest edition of the *Weekly Reader*, in which we got to vote! I'd checked the box next to McGovern's head. He looked so kind compared with that Nixon fellow.

"No one in our house votes Democratic!" my dad scolded. He was joking, of course, but I still felt ashamed, as if I'd just admitted I loved macramé plant holders or hippies. How could I have been so wrong? I should have voted for Nixon! My parents later did, and he won. Meanwhile, I slunk off, feeling as though I'd committed a crime. (As the incumbent president soon would.) In my mind, I picture myself crumpling up the paper, my first foray into politics a horrid mistake.

Lizzie wasn't interested in getting involved in the 2012 election, but what if she had wanted to volunteer for Romney and Ryan? Do my husband and I truly encourage dissent with Lizzie? Would I have driven her to help with that campaign? I happily drove all over eastern Pennsylvania when she wanted to canvass for Obama in 2008. We meandered door-to-door, encouraging registered Democrats to vote. Would I hold the pamphlets quite as cheerfully if she supported a different candidate? I don't think so. I would drive her, of course, just not nearly as happily. But I honestly can't see Lizzie embracing views drastically different from ours. Right now, she values support for education and health care, declares the growing income disparity "unfair," and is concerned about protecting the environment.

And how to explain "values" and the coded semantics of political language to a kid? During a recent local election, Lizzie and I studied the voters' guide, which was filled with names and photos of candidates and blurbs about their positions on various issues. One candidate had written she supported "family values." I muttered, "Uh-oh. I'll stay away from her."

"But Mom, aren't family values a good thing? Our family has values," Lizzie said, puzzled.

I tried to explain that those "family values" were often quite different from ours.

If she someday embraces "family values," the Tea Party, or other right-wing philosophies, could it damage my relationship with her? Although I try to understand my parents' political beliefs, I don't. When I see what Newsmax "article" or *Wall Street Journal* editorial my father "likes" on Facebook, or glance at a photo taken a few years back of my folks dressed as McCain and Palin for Halloween, I feel physically sick. Sometimes it's hard to have even simple conversations with them. Even the most innocent pleasantry, like "Nice weather," could spiral out of control if I let my adolescent desire to debate take over. Because if my dad says, "I bet you guys are happy you're not back east this winter. All that snow in New York." I'm tempted to mutter something about climate change, but instead I bite my tongue and say, "Yes, in Portland we don't have to shovel rain."

It sometimes seems my parents and I are as divided as Congress, neither side understanding the other's point of view. But when I'm around them, I somehow morph into a sullen sixteen-year-old with no power, whose views are considered childish. I want to engage, to discuss topics calmly with them, but my emotions knock any possibility of cool-headed debate out of the way. All my facts and statistics—

the cornerstone of rational debate—get gummed together in my mouth by raw emotion, and I manage to get out only incoherent raw rantings. And if history is any indication of the future, I'm doomed to repeat myself.

I wish I could debate issues calmly, like my husband does. Or maybe I should take a lesson from Lizzie. The truth is, she can teach me a thing or two about politics. Instead of getting scorched by the heat of the moment, as I do, she's cool and collected. She listens intently. And every so often, an innocent question she asks will sum up any prejudice succinctly:

"Why don't Grammy and Grampy want Charlie's moms to get married? That's not fair."

I began to offer her a halfhearted reply about how different people believe different things and then stopped myself before summarizing, "You know, you're right."

"LIZZIE WANTS TO BE FRIENDS ON FACEBOOK."

I was scrolling through my Face-book news feed when Lizzie came into my office and stood behind me.

"When can I get Facebook? I'm thirteen now," she asked, adding, "And, you know, it's legal for kids to get Facebook once they turn thirteen."

"You're right. It's 'legal' now, but it's still up to parents to decide," I said. "Let me think about it and talk to Jeff."

❋ ❋ ❋

I knew this was coming. Some of Lizzie's friends already had Facebook accounts, and she'd recently become curious about mine. ("Jeff, Mom's on Facebook again!")

Social media allows me to keep in touch with old friends and to post a scrapbook's worth of photos of Lizzie for family across the country and on the other side of the world, plus discuss issues and share information with people who aren't in the room. Since I work at home, I think of it as my little coffee break—a chance to interact with people for a few minutes instead of staring at my walls or talking to my coffee mug. While for me it may make staying connected easier, for teens social media can mean opening doors to all sorts of potential problems: cyberbullying, inappropriate posts, new ways to waste time, and the equivalent of inviting strangers into a home. On the other hand, it's an easy way for Lizzie to stay in touch with some of her friends from when we lived in New York and from summer camp, in addition to communicating by e-mail, Gchat, and Skype.

Before we okayed Facebook for Lizzie, we asked her what she knew about Internet safety and talked to her about being responsible regarding the posting of sensitive information.

"We learned about all that in fifth grade," Lizzie told us, sighing. "I'm very careful."

She is. When she plays games online, she always asks before she gives out personal data. She deletes junk e-mail and doesn't open attachments on forwarded e-mail. I don't think I have to worry about her clicking links promising "See Who Viewed Your Facebook Profile!" or "Get a Free iPad!" But posting online bits of her life is different. What if she inadvertently posted the name of her school or a photo of her house, with the address visible? Then there's always the possibility of a young teen posting without thinking it through: "I can't stand [name]." "English class really sucked today." I truly can't picture Lizzie writing anything like that (she loves English class and seems to have a natural filter the size of an aquifer), but as a parent, you just never know.

Facebook isn't the only online site to be concerned about. There's Twitter and whatever new social media all the kids will be using by the time you read this, on whatever new computing device is in vogue in the near future. Remember when experts recommended that parents keep the family computer in a central location to monitor their children's online life? That advice seems as quaint and outdated as tucking a shiny dime in your purse in case you need to call home when being courted by a boy. Lizzie takes my laptop into her room for homework. When I upgrade my laptop, we'll probably give her my old computer. Meanwhile, she uses her iPod to check her e-mail, video chat with friends, and surf the Internet—and could easily use it to access Facebook, bypassing parental checkpoints. Technology is moving faster than the advice given to parents about how to navigate it, and many young teens unintentionally circumvent the computer safety rules of old—many have tablets or smart phones, allowing for more unsupervised Internet freedom.

Not long after Jeff and I agreed Lizzie could get an account, I scrolled down my page's news feed. A friend's fifteen-year-old daughter smiled at me from a photo. Camera in hand, she'd shot a self-portrait through the mirror, wearing a smile and not a whole lot else. Her 675 friends, real and virtual, posted glowing comments about how she looked in her tiny bikini. She thanked them or "liked" what they said. I was stunned. Not only because I know this child—she'll forever be emblazoned in my mind as a darling and precocious five-year-old—but because my thirteen-year-old daughter was about to get her own account.

My first thought (after the shock subsided) was, *I'm glad she's got a positive body image.* Then I concluded that it's most likely something else entirely. I suspect many children post pictures like this because they're insecure and trying to see themselves through the eyes of others. I get this. As a teen I was myopic; others' eyes lent a clarity that my hazel ones didn't have. But this is exactly what I'm scared of—I would be horrified if Lizzie one day did something similar.

I have mixed feelings about "friending" children, too. When my teenage niece sent me a friend request, I informed my sister, wanting to get her okay before I accepted. I told her I'd been friended by a few other friends' children, but I always checked with their parents first. It's not that I post steamy photos or racy material, but occasionally virtual conversations can veer in non-PG-rated directions. My sister assured me that her daughter had probably seen far worse than anything I would ever post. She said she monitors her daughter's posts and has made her take down a few inappropriate comments.

* * *

When Lizzie joined Facebook, she sent me a friendship request. Of course I accepted, but I wondered: Shouldn't there be more of a firewall between parents and kids? How much of our children's lives do we really need to know? Isn't privacy and independence a good thing? Can we become too mired in each other's lives? And frankly, I don't want to watch my language or police my postings/friends' comments knowing my daughter might have her ears pressed to the computer, to eavesdrop on my virtual conversations. I value my privacy. And I think Lizzie should have hers. I suppose I could alleviate the fear that she'll see inappropriate postings by setting up a "family friendly" subgroup. But I don't want to bother with that. And I assume Lizzie could set her privacy settings so I'd see only what she wanted me to. I truly don't think I'd have a problem with that. As with most of our parenting, my husband and I tell Lizzie we assume she will do the right thing. If she proves otherwise, then she loses our trust—and we tell her it's hard to rebuild that. She seems to get it. We trust her to make good life choices, real and virtual.

So we're trying to find the balance: a bit of a firewall is good, but too much of one isn't. When I was a child, there wasn't just a firewall between my parents and me—it was the

Great Firewall of China, undulating and impenetrable, stretching for many miles. I shared very little of my business with them. And to ensure my secrets stayed classified, my best friend and I discussed them in a made-up language both of us had learned as young teens. We were fluent in Gibberish.

Older and younger teens test boundaries. As a teen, I didn't just test limits; I think I earned an A-plus in pushing them. But with Facebook and the Internet, childish "mistakes" can be engraved forever in the ether.

* * *

I fell hard for my first real boyfriend. I chatted with him late into the night on my pink Princess phone, the one I kept in my bedroom and dragged around like a leashed dog through the shag carpet, here to my red vinyl beanbag chair, there to my bed. I was convinced I was in love and that one day we'd get married and stroll off, hand in hand, into the sunset. Our relationship wasn't based on love and mutual respect, though—it was based on control and manipulation. It was as if I'd somehow found the perfect dysfunctional starter relationship, one that worked with my insecurity to make me feel so protected and loved when I was with him and sink further into self-doubt when I wasn't.

It's not all that difficult to talk a girl into things when she's insecure and desperately wants to please. My boyfriend, in his low, sexy voice, told me he missed me deeply—even though we saw each other every single day—and wanted a little something to remind him of me when we weren't together. A lock of hair or a wallet-size class photo wouldn't do. Instead, I posed for him. Naked. He held my hand as we watched the Polaroid develop—it was probably more so than I was. As will happen when one is young and in an unhealthy relationship, we broke up and got back together and broke up and so on. When we broke up for what would be the last time, he gave the photo to my parents. He didn't threaten me with it; he just did it to embarrass me and to scandalize them. There was a knock on the door to my room. I remember the look of shock and disappointment on my parents' faces as they held the picture out to me. They ripped it up. I can still feel the pure relief that the photo was away from my ex-boyfriend and was gone forever, mingled with the knowledge that I'd let them down yet again. And disappointing my parents was pretty much my default mode as a teenager.

* * *

If today's technology existed then, I have no doubt I would have been stupid enough to pose for a phone pic for my boyfriend. And I'm sure he would have had no compunction about sharing it with hundreds of his Facebook friends or his entire e-mail list. This is the world Lizzie is entering: one with not just technology and its dangers, but technology combined with adolescence, experimentation, first loves, and first mistakes.

There used to be a learning curve for stupid teenage mistakes, one that it was possible to zigzag around. Now, with technology, it's easy to go slamming into the curve at full speed, flip over and wipe out, getting hurt permanently in the process. We try to get that message across to Lizzie the best we can but we also occasionally monitor her online activity since she is still a child.

And Lizzie's Facebook account? Turns out we didn't need to worry (yet, anyway). I recently asked her how she liked it.

She thought for about five seconds before responding, "You know, Facebook is actually kind of boring."

"DO YOU BELIEVE IN GOD?"

'll make a peanut butter and matzo sandwich since I can't have bread," Lizzie said, grabbing a knife from the drawer to have a Passover snack. My daughter, at thirteen, has decided she's a little bit Jewish. Her ancestors, Irish Catholics, are as Jewish as I am, but the only dad she's ever really known, Jeff, is a nonreligious Jew. And as an agnostic ex-Catholic married to him, I don't mind at all that Lizzie is experimenting with religion. But I do hope it's not habit-forming.

Lizzie has been trying on bits and pieces of religions for years now, discarding each after a little wear. One night a few years ago, as we read a book together about the decidedly secular Nancy Drew, she asked out of the blue if I believed in God. As she snuggled into the crook of my arm, chewing on a strand of dark blond hair, she waited for an answer.

"Well, some people believe in God," I answered, carefully putting on the same serious but accessible voice I'd used to answer previous uncomfortable questions about where babies come from and why there are homeless families.

"Do *you* believe?" Lizzie said, stressing the "you" so there was no getting around it. I had to answer.

"No, I don't," I said as concern creased her face.

Should I have lied and just said I believed? After all, God seems to be embedded in almost every nook and cranny of this country. Way back in kindergarten, the Pledge of Allegiance told her she's part of one nation under God. Lizzie sees friends and family go to church or temple each week and smiles at the store clerk who tells her to "have a blessed day." Giant decorated trees and huge menorahs are everywhere she looks each December (rather, menorahs used to be everywhere—then we moved to Portland). Every time I dig through my wallet to find bills to buy a gallon of milk, or anything at all, I see His name.

There are chunks of society that say if you don't believe in God, you're a bad person. Will Lizzie intuit that she's bad if she doesn't believe—or that her mother is? Or is it okay to tell her what I believe: It's a superstition that many people believe but I don't, and that, to me, it seems like mystical make-believe. Maybe I should take what I like about religion—the moral and ethical bits—and drop the rest, my own personal ecumenical smorgasbord. I'll take one Golden Rule and seven of the Ten Commandments, please, and hold the mortal sin and transubstantiation.

* * *

My disenchantment with religion started long ago, when I went to Mass each Sunday. I wore frilly dresses that my mother had carefully laid out the night before and white acrylic tights that itched my legs and sagged uncomfortably as I sat, week after week, on the polished dark wooden pew, standing and sitting on command, but not really listening to the priest. I chanted when everyone else did, but instead of meditating on God's glory, I'd flip through the hymnal and wiggle on the hard wooden seat. After my First Communion, as the wafer dissolved slowly on my tongue, I realized that to me it was just a wafer. The church didn't fill me with the Holy Ghost, just the feeling it was a scam. There wasn't one single event that made me feel this way—just a series of Sundays and something deep in me. I was a closeted agnostic at age six. But I kept going.

When I was a teenager, I'd attend each Sunday morning, despondently studying the other teenagers, potheads, and cheerleaders. A cheerleader who at school strutted past with a flip of her perfectly coiffed hair as if I didn't exist now smirked a fake lip-glossed smile at me and shook hands when the priest told us to offer each other a sign of peace. As soon as Mass was over, the détente ended and everyone went back to their roles, the weekly pretend play over. I smoked dope with the potheads, and the cheerleaders ignored lesser girls.

High school also taught me how malleable faith could be—religious beliefs seemed as steadfast and unbendable as tinfoil. After losing my religion as a teen, I lost my virginity and got pregnant. My parents, avowed Catholics, took me to the clinic for an abortion without a second thought. We didn't even consider any other alternative for more than twenty seconds—and thanks be to my parents for that. But it crystallized the feeling that religion was full of hypocrisies—and you could twist it and turn it to fit your needs. I still went with my parents to church, though, weekly. I didn't ask them not to go and they didn't tell me to go; it was expected that I go, so I did. But as soon as I left home, I left my religion without a second glance. During my twenties and thirties, I gave as much thought to religion as I did to my 401(k)—pretty much none. But in my mid-forties, I found myself back in church for the first time in decades.

My forty-year-old cousin and her two young children had been killed. There aren't words to explain the awfulness of what happened, but here are a few to describe it: It was late. It was dark. My cousin was driving with her two kids tucked safely into their car seats. Something happened and the car hit a tree. It burst into flames. Everyone died.

Red electric candles flickered in the corners and incense burned my nose and eyes. Flowers and tiny white coffins were wheeled into the church and placed next to the larger coffin—children snuggled next to their mother in death, as in life. All around, mourners sobbed. My cousin's husband was lost to his grief, his entire family gone in less time than it takes to say three Hail Marys. What can you say to someone drowning in misery? And how can anything you say possibly make it better? It can't.

The priest's words, meant to console the family, fell flat to me. Everything seemed like a false comfort offered for such bottomless loss. Part of me wants to be able to tell Lizzie her second cousins are in a better place, to buffer her from the sadness of children dying. But it feels like a lie. So what do I say when other people tell her they're in heaven? Do I stare straight ahead while she looks quizzically at me to find out if I believe that, too? What's wrong with a white lie to help ease grief? I fight the urge to answer like a therapist. ("Are my second cousins in heaven?" "What do you think?")

I feel comfortable with what I believe about not believing, but I still find it hard to talk to Lizzie about it. I want to let her know my opinions but also give her the space to decide for herself and not have her beliefs trailer-hitched to mine. So we read my old children's Bible, Greek myths, and Native American creation stories. And she brings what we talk about into her everyday life.

"Look! It's the woman falling from the sky!" Lizzie shouted after she'd tossed my old Baby Tender Love into the air and gravity did its work. We'd just read the Iroquois creation story *The Woman Who Fell from the Sky*, which we'd picked up at the library after kindergarten had finished for the day.

When Lizzie was in third grade, she toted my old children's Bible everywhere for a few weeks as she played "Colonial child." (They were studying that time period in school.)

"Kids back then learned to read from the Bible. And I'm a Colonial child," she said as she strolled around the house one day after school, wearing a hoopskirt we'd bought the previous year from a neighbor who was a Colonial reenactor.

In fifth grade, on a Greek and Roman mythology binge, fueled by the writer Rick Riordan and a bookcase full of beautifully illustrated myth anthologies, Lizzie asked me, "Who's your favorite Greek god or goddess?" Without waiting for my answer, she said, "Mine's Athena."

Lizzie's dad tells her the story about Moses at Passover and about the Maccabees and the oil when we eat latkes at Hanukkah. I tell her about Jesus during Christmas and Easter. But I feel compelled to stress to her that these are myths that some people believe. And is it hypocritical on my part to even talk about Moses and Jesus? To have a tree? To search for eggs? To eat latkes?

Lizzie is sifting and sorting and exploring theology in her own way. She and her dad started their own religion, Dalala, after her fish Sparkly died. It involves lighting a candle for all the people or animals who've died in the past year— so they can come back as babies. It also involves eating pancakes. It's a religion that only needs to be observed once annually, on March 26th, and we've done so for eight years now. It sounds as plausible as anything I grew up with.

So, each Dalala and every other day of the year, Lizzie has the room to believe what she wants. I taught her to brush her teeth, to look both ways before crossing the street, and to think about religion from a historical standpoint. She's a kind and thoughtful child, a living Golden Rule. And if one day she decides to "get" religion, I'll love her and forgive her. Especially if pancakes are involved.

"CAN I GET AMERICAN EAGLE JEANS?"

At fifth-grade pickup one day when we were still living back in New York, a friend approached the car, looking exhausted. This was understandable considering she'd just spent the day with eight children stuffed in her minivan, chaperoning a field trip.

"I'm so glad I have a boy," she said.

I must have looked confused.

"Those girls," she whispered, jabbing her finger in the direction of three "popular" girls, "all they did was talk about *stuff* the entire time."

She made her voice high and mean-girl bitchy. "'Oh, you've got to get this kind of iPod.' 'Ew, that car is ugly—your mom drives the right car.' 'You have to get a pair of these boots.' It was unbelievable."

I asked what Lizzie and her friend, who are not in the popular crowd, did. And what about her son and his buddies?

"They sang along to the *Madagascar 2* soundtrack." She smiled.

I'm still a bit baffled how such rampant consumerism crept into a part of the Hudson Valley better known for organic farms, hippies, and New Age pursuits. Quite a few of the families at this school had moved to this idyllic corner of the world from New York City, looking to escape, among other things, out-of-control consumerism. If materialism lurked there, no place was safe from it.

Lizzie is now in middle school, and (so far, anyway) she doesn't seem overly interested in money and what it can buy. Although she enjoys picking out new clothes on occasion, she doesn't seem to care much about having the "right" clothing, shoes, or cell phone, and isn't worried about keeping up with the Joneses' kids. In fact, I don't think she's heard of them.

I realize that this could eventually change, and it may indeed be starting to, a little bit. She recently requested jeans from American Eagle, a store that markets to teens. We bought a pair. I like to think this purchase will help inoculate her against an obsession with consumer goods—that by getting one or two pairs of the "right" jeans and a closet full of "regular" clothes, she'll realize that a pair that is pricier than other jeans is a special treat and thus gain a sense of the value of money.

How can we help relatively nonmaterialistic adolescents navigate a society where it's viewed by many as necessary to have a closet crammed with the right jeans, shirts, and shoes? How can we help to keep them from falling prey to the lure of "stuff"? Is it possible for kids to learn to see beyond the gloss when consumerism is so ingrained? I think it's important to help Lizzie see the difference between needs and wants.

Why do some children seem far more enamored of material goods than others? I used to think it was television—that a steady diet of ads for Air Jordans and Bratz dolls fueled a yearning. But now that Lizzie is in middle school, I don't believe that's the case. Many of Lizzie's classmates were raised with no or limited television. Nor do I think that it's necessarily the parents, many of whom at Lizzie's school could be described as having limited interest in "things." To many in our neighborhood, material goods are items created on their sewing machines.

So where does it come from? It's almost as if some children are born with an innate sense of what goods are cool and, with that, a desire for them. And other kids want what the cool kids have. Could well-meaning parents be subconsciously affecting how their children view others with less? Perhaps steering young children away from a cheap pair of boots with an offhand, "Oh, those look like they'll fall apart quickly—let's find a better pair," or, "Let's try a different store, okay?" sends the message that some footwear is better than others. Possibly they avoid parking near an "ugly" car in the grocery store parking lot. Maybe their child overhears an offhand comment they make about the newer iPod being far superior to the older model. Could children become enamored of goods by osmosis? Thinking back to my actions and words over the years, I'm sure I've sent Lizzie an abundance of subliminal messages about material items.

Does the desire for the "right" things come from older siblings? Have the younger children perhaps learned what things are desirable from them? Or do we simply have an inborn love of the shiny and new?

For parents trying to avoid the pitfalls of unchecked materialism, it can sometimes feel as if they're shoving a finger in a dam to keep all the "wants" pressing on the other side from pouring through. But no matter how many fingers and toes are jammed in the crack, some keep seeping in.

My husband and I believe it's important not only to keep consumerism and materialism at bay but also to teach Lizzie how to handle her money. In not that many years, she'll be on her own in a world with virtually unlimited credit and a tempting array of, well, everything.

Right now, Lizzie enjoys trawling Amazon for what she calls "interesting" things. By that she means scrolling through the more than twenty-five thousand items having to do with Harry Potter or searching for books by British authors from the 1940s and '50s. She occasionally buys books but rarely spends her money on the "goods," the multitude of scarves, games, and other paraphernalia that have a connection, often tenuous, to Harry Potter. She peruses the site in the same way I used to sprawl on the brown-speckled shag carpet of our family room, Sears Wish Book opened in front of me, pen in hand. I'd carefully study the toys and games, circling the ones I'd love to have. There were many. Did I expect any of these to be waiting under the tree for me on Christmas morning? Not really—maybe one or two, if I was lucky and had left the catalog conveniently folded back to reveal the desired item and placed it somewhere my parents would be certain to see it, such as their bedside table or on their place mat. But it was a catalog that lived up to its name—I wished for things but didn't expect to actually get them, any more than I expected Ed McMahon to knock on my door one day with a giant check and a bouquet of balloons.

Lizzie may enjoy window-shopping on the computer screen, but she realizes looking isn't the same as buying. She knows we're not wealthy. We're not poor, but we certainly don't have endless funds for a closet full of the "right" clothes or her own iPhone or new laptop. And even if we did, I wouldn't want her to think that these are more important than a stroll through the park with our dogs on a Saturday afternoon or playing a rousing game of Blokus with her grandparents.

I think she understands. She came into my office one day after school when she first became interested in the year-round swim team.

"I can pay part of the monthly dues," she said earnestly.

I told her that was an incredibly nice offer, but she didn't need to do that.

"But I'll use some of my own money to help pay for my team suit," she declared as if the matter were settled.

My initial reaction was that there was no way I'd take money from our daughter, but then I thought about it and decided it was a great idea. She now has more of a personal stake in the suit and the team than if they were just given to her.

* * *

We've been working with Lizzie on money issues since the tooth fairy left a shiny Sacagawea dollar under her pillow in exchange for that first baby incisor. She dropped the coin into her ceramic piggy bank instead of rushing out and spending it on candy. Around that time, she also started getting an allowance, a minimal amount each week that she usually saved. When she was in elementary school, we went to the bank together to open a savings account in which she would regularly deposit birthday checks. We wanted the bank to be a regular part of her life from early on so she'd start to understand financial matters. But it's still a work in progress.

We visited recently so she could deposit a check from a multiday baby-sitting job, saving most of it and getting the rest in cash. I stood back as she attempted to do everything herself. After endorsing the back of the check, she waited in line for the teller.

"How do you want your bills?" the teller asked her.

"Huh?" she asked. She looked bewildered.

"Tens or a twenty?" he questioned.

"Oh, tens, please," she told him. Then she pocketed the money, looked toward me, smiled, and waved that she was ready to go.

As we walked outside into the summer afternoon's heat, I asked what had confused her.

"When he asked me how I wanted my money, I thought he wanted to know if I wanted wrinkled bills or crisp ones," she said.

* * *

Lizzie still has the same piggy bank sitting on her bookshelf, stuffed with bills from her allowance and baby-sitting. She saves more than she spends but takes money out to use for ice cream, iced mochas, or books. Right now, she seems to have achieved a good balance of saving and spending on larger special treats, such as a coveted necklace with its tiny silver keys. She can delay her gratification, something that, I hope, will help keep her solvent in the future and avoid the quicksand of credit card debt—she seems to be training herself to wait for what she desires.

I glanced into her room one evening as she was sitting at her desk, doing homework. A Life Saver was perched on the edge of a worksheet. I asked what she was doing.

"This is a reward for finishing math," she said, pointing to the orange circle.

She finished scribbling on the paper and looked up.

"All done," she declared, popping the candy in her mouth.

> "How do you type on this thing?"

> "Here, let me try."

Sometimes it seems as if Lizzie is the last young teen in America without her own cell phone. I know this is not true. Her friend Kate also doesn't have one.

Most of Lizzie's eighth-grade classmates have their own phones. Jeff and I have so far resisted—we don't believe Lizzie needs one yet. Whenever she bikes to the library or goes to the movies, she takes an old, pay-as-you-go phone we have just for these occasions. When she's back from the activity, she returns the phone. But even though Lizzie doesn't have her own phone, she seems to have an innate ability to use all different kinds of them.

Not long ago, Lizzie and I went out for a special mother/ daughter evening. I'd bought tickets to *Wicked*, which she had wanted to see, and we left our house early to have sushi before the event. As we were waiting for our fish to arrive, I took out my new smart phone to check what the parking garage's hours were since we were expecting a fairly late night. I pictured arriving back at the garage after the show and finding the gate locked, car trapped inside. I put on my reading glasses as I attempted to type on the small keyboard with fingers that suddenly seemed enormous.

"Oops," I said as I inadvertently clicked on a video link to a network news story about garages.

Lizzie wriggled in her chair and reached for the phone.

"Could I try?" she asked.

"Sure," I said. I handed it to her just as I was ready to toss it through the restaurant's plate glass window.

Her fingers flew as she typed, as if they'd been made to do so. She hadn't used this phone before but seemed instinctively to know exactly which buttons to press. Maybe this was from years of iPod use. Or maybe it's evolutionary growth: from early humanoid's use of hand axes and hammer stones to early teen's use of tiny keyboards.

My fingers are more stone age. On the relatively rare occasions when I send e-mail from my phone, out of necessity I keep it short. I have to. Still, my notes tend to look something like this: "Dud Carhy call?" Somehow Jeff is able translate this to "Did Cathy call?" Lizzie, though, can write long, complex messages to friends on her iPod's keyboard. I've seen her typing away and I've asked if she wanted to borrow my laptop for e-mail.

"No, Mom. I'm fine," she replied each time, continuing to type while talking.

Lizzie quickly found the information I needed about the parking garage. It was open late. We finished our dinner, paid the bill, and walked to the theater. While we were waiting for the show to start, Lizzie and I sent Jeff an e-mail for no other reason than to say hello (and we were bored). Then we turned off the phone and tucked it away in my bag. As the lights were turned down, a constellation of smart phones glowed around us as audience members posted status updates, sent messages to friends, and took and posted photos.

"I thought you weren't supposed to do that—in movies you can't," Lizzie whispered.

I quietly confirmed that it was rude.

Then we sat back in our seats and enjoyed a worry-free show, thanks to Lizzie's adeptness with the phone. Maybe one day I'll be as skillful. Or find a phone with giant buttons.

"DO THESE SHORTS MAKE MY BUTT LOOK BIG?"

Lizzie emerged from the dressing room and looked in the mirror. She spun around, glancing at her backside in the mirror, and paused, frowning.

"Ugh. Do these shorts make my butt look big?" she asked.

My heart sank. This was a new question, one I had suspected was eventually coming but so far had managed to avoid. We were in a store that specialized in juniors' fashion, featuring pulsating pop tunes and tables stacked with colorful clothing—the type of place where both the music and the outfits would be stale within a few months. Not that that mattered to Lizzie, whose fashion sense is more sensible than fashionable. She had riffled through the piles of jean shorts and grabbed a few, marked with plastic strips emblazoned with "2" and "4" in large print, scarlet numbers seemingly designed to shame.

"I will definitely try on the 2 first," she said.

Lizzie, always quick to pick up on the "right" grade to receive in school, found it easy to tell from the pictures of models on the walls and the way the clothes were stacked, with the smaller sizes front and center and larger sizes tucked out of the way, which sizes were the "right" ones.

Even though I'd told her that sizes don't mean a lot and that it seems I'm a different size in each store, she had changed into the smaller pair. As she looked at her backside in the mirror, she grimaced and asked if the shorts made her butt look big. I said they didn't; they were just too small.

"I'll try the 4s," she said, pulling the stall door shut behind her.

As I loitered near the changing room with another mother, I started to think about how Lizzie has always felt confident of her body and had a relatively good sense of her body self-image, but it seems to be shifting now that she's a teen. When she was younger, she would ask me to admire her muscles as she announced, "I'm a strong girl!" She happily ate what she called her "growing food" before devouring her dessert with gusto. We've never subscribed to the type of fashion magazine that offers a skewed sense of femininity, the kind that is filled with page after page of airbrushed photos of severely thin, doll-faced young women doing pretty much nothing other than wearing clothing and putting on too much makeup. Instead, she prefers magazines with articles about girls who write novels or build their own birdhouses. Anyway, Lizzie has never been especially interested in fashion. For years, her "style" has consisted almost exclusively of jeans paired with whatever T-shirt is at the top of her dresser drawer. It's almost as if she's making up for her early childhood—she spent her preschool years prancing around in a series of frilly dresses (also sizes 2, 4, 6) and sparkly shoes. Those early years were the last time she reveled in "feminine" attire. In fourth grade, she flipped through the pages of *Girls' Life* magazine at the library and then flung it down. "Ew, it's for girly-girls—it's all about clothes and boring stuff." I felt like planting a big wet kiss on her cheek. But her shift toward this newer, more "grown-up" version of body image frightens me. It's a developmental milestone of the most unwelcome kind.

* * *

I remember my milestone, my precise before and after moment. The summer I was eleven, our family visited my grandparents in Missouri. One especially hot and humid day, my younger sister and I stood in the living room in our swimsuits, clutching water toys, and waited for an adult to drive us to the swimming pool. My grandmother turned to my mom and said, "Sue's looking a little chunky." It was as if I weren't there. But I was standing right near my mom, clutching an inflatable green cow ring for the pool. Suddenly I felt puffy and full of air, too, like a living water toy. My grandmother certainly didn't make the comment in a cruel way; she just stated it as a fact. A fact I wasn't previously aware of. I'd never given my weight a single minute of thought. I wore clothes my mom bought or made for me and occasionally selected my own—things like animal-emblazoned T-shirts and bright yellow bell-bottoms from Sears or JCPenney. I'd never thought of myself as fat or as thin. I just was. But that all changed with my grandmother's comment. I looked down at my stomach. Maybe she was right. Maybe I *was* chunky. Later, back at my grandmother's house, I packed that comment away—along with the "dinner" that was served on the large kitchen table. Lunch at my grandparents' was the biggest meal of the day, with dishes such as sliced chicken, corn on the cob, potato salad, and my favorite: fluorescent Jell-O "salad," molded into gravity-defying shapes with bits of American cheese and shredded carrot floating in it. We drank

Kool-Aid from colorful aluminum tumblers that lent a vaguely metallic tang to the drink. All of it was delicious, and seconds were not discouraged.

During the next few years, I thought about my weight only occasionally. I was chubby compared with my skinny mom and swizzle-stick-thin younger sister. (When I see pictures from back then, it's clear my mom was frighteningly skinny. She'd had a hard time with the food in Indonesia and had been hospitalized for hepatitis A.) So I wouldn't think at all about being chunky, whether or not my blue striped T-shirt and shorts felt a bit too tight. Our family would go to the Purple Submarine, the only pizza parlor in Jakarta at the time, order a large pepperoni pie, and eat as many slices as we could. I remember the proud feeling when I finally was able to match my dad, eating three large slices.

Thus began my "it's complicated" relationship with food. I'd fret about being "chubby." Or I wouldn't think about it and I'd stuff myself, like a piñata, beyond full.

When we moved back from Indonesia to Louisiana, my relationship with food stayed slightly dysfunctional. The scary thing, though, was that almost every teenage girl I met had a similar convoluted relationship with food. This was the new normal. In junior high school, my only friend in seventh grade would not eat around other people. She brought her lunch each day but would eat only if we were sitting alone, together, in the nook of the home ec building. She'd turn around, facing away from me, and cautiously nibble her American cheese sandwich. If our usual spot was occupied by other kids, she wouldn't eat lunch. The following year, another friend and I twisted Saran Wrap around our stomachs at a sleepover after polishing off a bag of Cheetos. We'd heard this was a good way to lose water weight. Instead, we looked like leftover snacks.

In eleventh grade, I became skinny thanks to a little trick I discovered called "skipping lunch." I brought money to school each day to buy food in the cafeteria, but I didn't. Instead, I gave it to my first boyfriend. After school, he'd drive us to Burger King in his ancient primer-dotted Audi and buy a burger or large fries with my lunch money. The smell of those hot, crispy fries made me drool with anticipation, but I didn't eat even one. Because I knew deep down that one delicious fry could be a gateway drug—it might lead to a massive binge on fried foods. And I couldn't have that. My life would be so much better if I could just lose those last five pounds.

After one such afternoon of denying myself even a single french fry, we drove to my boyfriend's house, where one of his buddies, a skinny pothead sprouting a crown of frizzy hair—a boy no one would remotely confuse with a fashion model—suggested that I should ride a bike, as perhaps my butt, which was flat, would benefit. Why did I immediately feel that I should grab the nearest bicycle, hop on it, and pedal twenty miles? Why did the words of this relatively unattractive teenager seem more important to me at sixteen than my eyes in the mirror? Why did I value a virtual stranger's opinion more than my own? Was my self-esteem that lacking? Why, yes, of course it was! But I also think many teenage girls—today as well as back then—seem to have a body blindness. We're so worried about how we appear to others that we can't see how we really are. I know this was the case with me. And it was pervasive in high school. I don't remember anyone at all who felt confident about her body.

My parents certainly didn't consciously add to this. Though I remember my grandmother's words vividly (Missouri accent included), my parents never said anything about my weight. We were never forbidden food. Most nights we ate family dinners—balanced meals planned, with military precision, weeks ahead of time, the menus scribbled in a notebook, with a list of needed ingredients. (Today I plan our menu each evening by opening the refrigerator and seeing what's inside.) They kept junk food in the house, but not too much of it. Apples and oranges were always in the crisper. Occasionally they took us out for fast food, but we enjoyed everything in moderation.

I don't ever want Lizzie to catch the body blindness I had. Like my parents, we've never forbidden any food in our house, and Lizzie eats what she wants. We don't really buy junk food or soda and have a refrigerator stuffed with fruit and vegetables. If we're at the supermarket and Lizzie sees something she'd like to try, we'll usually purchase it. For example, when she was younger she wanted to try a certain dried potato chip–like product packaged in a can similar to those that hold tennis balls. We dropped a can into our cart, and she ate a few chips, but most of them ended up tossed into the trash. I suspect that if we'd forbidden it, this junk food would have reached a mythic allure. Instead, it reached the garbage bin. Lizzie loves sweets, of course, but seems to have an internal alarm, and if she's already had, say, ice cream at lunch, she won't request dessert after dinner. She's a snacker, and she'll eat when she's hungry, which these days seems to be every few hours. Right now, naan topped with a slice of Cheddar cheese is a favorite. She's rarely eaten fast food. (In fact, when she was little she thought it existed only in Arizona, where she ate it when she visited her grandparents.)

But, thinking back, I wonder if Lizzie has occasionally seemed a little too concerned with her weight. At the doctor's office for well-child visits, she took delight at being told she was on the lighter side. "I weigh less than most girls!" she said as if it were an Olympic event and she was going for the gold medal. Or, when she was a wisp of a preschooler and I'd lost weight thanks to the stress diet— my marriage had ended and, presto, I'd become a full-time single mom—Lizzie snuggled into my lap as I sat at my desk, announcing proudly, "We're little, Mommy."

Have I somehow inadvertently colored how she sees herself? All those times I look in the mirror when trying on dresses, sucking in my stomach and curling my face into a mask of disgust before catching myself. Has she overheard me say to my husband, "I need to go for a run," after I've had a big meal? At our local pool, when I'm reading in the shade, wearing a sundress or towel over my suit, is this sending a nonverbal message to her that I'm embarrassed by my body?

Even though I try not to do these things, I'm certain that I do. And Lizzie watching me watching myself in the mirror has to affect what she sees when she peers into it. So I try to balance what I know I do and say with setting a good example of living healthily, by running or bicycling frequently for fun. We'll take long walks together to our favorite café to split a chocolate-chip cookie. I make a point of never saying, "I can have this because I exercised." I don't ever want Lizzie sucked into the crazed diet math and its contorted calculus of calories. I want her to feel comfortable to grab whatever size jean shorts she wears, try them on, and decide it's the shorts, rather than her body, that are the wrong fit.

"DO YOU DRINK WINE EVERY NIGHT?"

Hair damp from her bath and dressed in fleece pajamas decorated with snowflakes, Lizzie padded into the kitchen and watched, disapprovingly, as I poured some pinot noir into a wineglass.

"Mom, do you drink wine every night?" she asked.

I glanced down at the red liquid. I didn't have to think to answer that one.

"Pretty much. But I rarely have more than one glass a night," I answered.

"We learned in school that alcohol is a drug," Lizzie said earnestly, as if she'd just caught me loitering in a back alley, jonesing for a fix. "And did you know it's a poison?" she added.

I told her that was true, but it was a legal drug for adults and it was fine as long as they drank responsibly. I mentioned that some doctors have said a little red wine each night is supposed to be good for grown-ups. I added that there are people, like my friend Amy, who can't or shouldn't drink, because they have an illness that makes it impossible to stop after one or two. (Amy is open about her alcoholism;

her children are aware of it.) I agreed that alcohol is indeed a poison and that it's possible to get very sick and even die from drinking too much. I told her it wasn't uncommon to read about college students dying from alcohol poisoning.

"Mom, *everyone* knows about alcoholism and that too much alcohol can kill you. We learned about that in school, too," Lizzie said, clearly exasperated with my ignorance of what's taught in school.

I told her I was glad she was learning this in school and added that when I was a kid, my school didn't teach about drugs and alcohol. I asked if she'd ever seen me have more than a glass at home. She had not. I asked her if she'd ever seen me drive after a glass of wine. She had not. I told her some people drink too much and some drive after drinking, which is extremely dangerous.

❋ ❋ ❋

Lizzie has seen me drink wine regularly for years. Back when she was four, we walked up our street in Brooklyn one evening after dinner to meet a friend at a café for a cookie (for her) and a glass of wine (for me).

"Mommy loves wine!" she shouted for the entire neighborhood to hear as she skipped next to me on the sidewalk, holding my hand.

I bowed my head and smiled sheepishly as we passed a woman who was pushing a stroller in the other direction. She remained expressionless, thank goodness, because I was mortified enough for the two of us. Was she poker-faced because she was embarrassed for me or because she thought I was setting a bad example? *Was* I setting a bad example? I like to think I'm setting a good example, showing how an adult drinks wine responsibly. Or could that just be a convenient excuse?

When I meet friends for dinner or a chat at night, I often have a glass of wine or beer. I've always been forthright with Lizzie about this and have certainly never hidden it as a mom I know did, waiting for her daughter to go to sleep before she would pour herself a glass. How should I handle the old "Do what I say and not what I do" now that Lizzie is nearing the age of experimentation, if and when she tries alcohol? And what should I tell her, if anything, about my own wildly experimental years?

Back when I was in high school, I experimented so much that I'm surprised I didn't receive extra credit from our school's science department. I sampled my first beer near the end of ninth grade, after swim practice one hot spring evening. I had gone out with a few kids from our team. The boy who organized the outing was older—as a senior, he seemed terribly mature. He invited a few girls from the team to take a ride in his pickup truck, which was jacked up on large wheels. As a rather shy girl with the nickname "Mack Truck" (I had big shoulders), I was thrilled to have been asked. Inside, I rolled down the passenger window in a futile attempt to cool off. I don't remember if he had a fake ID or bought it on his own (seventeen was pretty close to eighteen, then the legal drinking age in Louisiana), but the boy procured some beer. He pulled a can from the six-pack and offered it to us. The other girls each took one and so did I, nonchalantly, I hoped, as if a cold brew were as normal to me after swim practice as a Little Debbie Nutty Bar. My heart pounded as I popped open the flip-top lid and foam fizzed up. I tentatively took a sip and gagged. But it was cold and Louisiana nights were hot. I took another swallow. Even though I had less than half a can, I felt dizzy, more, I suspect, from the idea of beer than from the actual alcohol.

Even though I didn't really enjoy it, there was something liberating about that first beer, and over the next year, it led to other beers and then to other types of alcohol, including those favorite men of the South, Jack Daniel's and Jim Beam. There was an unfortunate run-in with something called Southern Comfort, which may have been southern but was not comfortable at all.

I drank alcohol back then for the same reason that, a few years later, I smoked pot. I wanted to escape from my life in a small town where I felt out of place. I was desperately shy and socially inept, and these two magical substances transformed me into a "normal kid," one who fit in. When I drank, I didn't immediately second-guess what I'd just said, as I usually did. I was funny! I was charming! The reality, however, was that I quickly segued from Witty Sue to Dimwitted Sue and from what I thought was life of the party to practically lifeless.

My friends and I were curious to try new things—we drank both wine and whiskey the same way: quickly, while wincing. We sampled all the different liquids in my parents' glass-door cabinet. The only one we left alone was the horribly sweet cordial in an intricately molded glass bottle. I believe no one had had any of it since 1965.

In eleventh grade, my parents somehow realized that my friends and I were raiding their liquor cabinet. They marked the liquid's level on the bottles' labels with a pen. My friends and I, always enterprising, topped off the bottles with water after sampling, hoping my folks wouldn't notice that their rum had changed from a dark, maple syrup–like hue to something more closely resembling apple juice. If they did, they didn't say anything.

I have the feeling that some of Lizzie's contemporaries are already experimenting. I've read comments referring to alcohol on the (very public) Facebook pages of classmates from Lizzie's old school. If they're not experimenting, some of them are clearly romanticizing it. At least the schools recognize this and discuss the problem. Still, I am happy the drinking age is twenty-one. I would be happier if the drinking age were raised to twenty-three, although the illegality of it had no impact on my teenage drinking, as I told Lizzie this one night when we were talking about teen drinking and driving at the dinner table, after a friend's brother got his learner's permit.

"Did you try alcohol when you were a teenager?" she asked.

I had to think for a second about how to answer her, but I also had the feeling she already knew the answer.

"Yes," I told her, "but I was really too young and I couldn't handle it and it made me sick. I wish I'd waited to try it." I left out pretty much everything else.

"Oh," Lizzie answered. She didn't seem surprised or shocked. Just satisfied with her fact-finding mission.

Jeff, who made his own wine in high school (the *Whole Earth Catalog* had a simple recipe), asked Lizzie what she would do if she was at a party where kids were drinking alcohol and they offered her a drink, maybe even tried to pressure her into doing it.

"I'd just say, 'No, thanks.' Or maybe, 'Drinking's not my thing,'" she said.

Will these responses come as easily when she's not sitting around the table with her parents, but hanging out with her friends? I have no idea. Right now she loves rules, and teen drinking breaks those rules. This, I'm sure, will change. I hope she tells us when she tries it, which I am pretty sure despite her denials she will do in the upcoming years.

The good news is that the root causes of my rebellion aren't lurking in Lizzie. She's in a very different place from where I was as an adolescent, far happier with herself and her life. She feels comfortable bringing up subjects she's curious about or that bother her. As a child, I would rather have done the Hustle through town decked out in bunny ears and a grass skirt than plop down on the sofa and discuss boyfriend problems, weight issues, or teen drinking with my parents.

With Lizzie, it's not just about discussing the dangers of alcohol, it's about keeping the lines of communication open regarding herself and what she's going through. Will that stop her from taking a drink? I doubt it, but it might prevent her from doing so for the wrong reasons, and it may lessen the chance that she will become a binge drinker.

Maybe it will help her avoid learning the hard way what can happen with too much alcohol, whether it's binge drinking, alcohol poisoning, or drunk driving.

"Has anyone in your school tried alcohol?" Jeff asked during our dinner conversation about drinking.

"I don't think so. We're just kids," Lizzie said. She sounded slightly unsure, though.

"You know, during the next few years, I bet some of your classmates will try alcohol," I said.

"Well, *I'm* not going to," Lizzie assured us.

Jeff and I looked at each other and then at Lizzie.

"Kiddo, I wouldn't necessarily be so sure about that. I hope not, but sometimes it'll be around and it can be hard to say no if your friends are all drinking," Jeff told her.

"I'd definitely never binge drink, because you can die," Lizzie informed us. This, she sounded certain about.

"Binge drinking, riding with someone who's been drinking, driving while you've been drinking—they can all kill kids," I said, adding that I'd known someone in high school who, while I was in college, died driving while drunk.

Lizzie studied Wally, the goldendoodle, curled by her feet.

Because Lizzie likes rules, sometimes I fear she actually listens too well. We want her to use her own reasoning, not just check off an item on a list of dos and don'ts. Will she? I hope so. Her life, and the lives of her friends, may depend on it.

"THEY TOLD ME THEY NEEDED SPACE."

Lizzie was unusually quiet one day after school. Most days, she chatters excitedly about her day the entire way home and I nod along or (occasionally) wish for earplugs. I asked what was up.

"I'm just tired," she said, covering her mouth as she yawned theatrically. She does many things well, but I don't see an Academy Award in her future.

Once home, she pulled out a dining room chair and sat next to me while I flipped through a magazine.

"They told me they needed space," she said, words bursting out and colliding into one another. Her face was a mask of misery.

"They" were four of her supposed friends who had told her at lunch that day they didn't want her to follow them into the bathroom. Certainly a reasonable request, except that they all suddenly had to pee at exactly the same time. Lizzie, assuming they were friends, got up to join them. They circled her like a wagon train and told her they needed space and that she should stay where she was. Just two months earlier, they'd come to Lizzie's birthday sleepover, where they all had stayed up until three AM, talking and watching a movie. And now this. Middle school can be a middle circle of hell for a quirky kid.

I revel in Lizzie's quirkiness. I love that she prefers the library to the mall ("I hate it, it's all the same") and that she used her own money to buy a Turkish phrase book ("I've always wanted to learn Turkish"). I adore the handwritten sign she tacked to her door, like the brass plaques on houses, that reads: "Historic site: Lizzie's room. Lizzie is the author of the Lilac Sommerset series and got the snow leopard off the endangered species list." I enjoy that she writes her own songs for the piano—one when she was younger was about the history of chocolate, starting with the Mayans, and recent tunes have included lyrics about climate change, world peace, and too much homework.

In addition to quirky interests, she's got some quirky personality traits that middle schoolers might not find so endearing: talking too much about her books, asking too many questions about whatever pops into her head, and speaking about things as if the other kids know what she's talking about. One girl looked confused when Lizzie used a description from a 1940s Enid Blyton book and remarked that the pizza they were eating was "simply wizard."

Lizzie is quirky. So was I when I was her age; so was her dad. The people I find most interesting as adults were unconventional as children. Usually at some point, as a new friend and I are moving from acquaintances to confidantes, the subject of middle or high school comes up, and we bond over our statuses as outsiders and outcasts. These are accomplished adults, in a variety of professions, although the majority seem to skew creative. I realize that my poll has a very small sample size, but still.

My friend Melanie, for example, a talented writer whose

books have been favorably reviewed in *The New York Times*, and I got together one evening. I mentioned a certain manipulative girl in Lizzie's class who had been giving her a hard time, telling her she was a best friend one minute and then gossiping about her to others the next. I told Melanie I was relieved Lizzie was "going toward the fun," avoiding this girl and finding children she considered "nice." This led our conversation back to when we were adolescents. As our kids sat nearby at their own table, playing Bananagrams, Melanie's voice cracked as she told me about attending a dance when she was in high school and desperately wishing she were elsewhere. She said she felt like an outsider, one who didn't dress like the other girls, who favored "country club" styles, complete with pearl chokers. As Melanie slouched against the wall, watching the other teenagers, she just *knew* she didn't belong at the dance and in her hometown. My friend Carla, who was a professor and then a creative professional, shook visibly as she talked about past mean girls. My husband vividly recalled not being invited to parties thrown by "friends" in eighth and ninth grade. ("On the other hand, I was an unpleasant little bastard," he said in his friends' defense.)

It's fascinating that all these years later when reviewing our pasts, we relive them: a jock's disparaging comment still rings in our ears; we feel the confusion and shame of being shunned by "friends"; our stomachs contract at the thought of navigating the cafeteria, trying to find a group, a place to belong. We talk about it more now that we have kids.

What is it about quirkiness that makes adults interesting but is reviled by middle and high schoolers? Do young teens desire safety in numbers and in sameness? After all, everything else in their lives is changing: their bodies, their moods, their relationships with their parents. It's a crossroads. They're no longer little kids, but sometimes the adults in their lives treat them that way. Perhaps they band together to gain a sense of control at a time when so much feels as though it's spinning out of it. And those who are quirky are relegated to the outside.

Even at Lizzie's artsy school where kids are "different," each group sports its unique but similar clothing and hairstyles, a studied nonconformity. The "cool" kids look as if they've stepped out of the pages of the same Urban Outfitters catalogs that have been showing up in our mailbox in Lizzie's name, unrequested. Those who are truly unconventional— the oddballs—don't necessarily fit in.

Lizzie not only marches to her own drum, she waltzes down the street to her own Beethoven piano concerto. And I know that's a good thing. But sometimes it feels as though I need to keep telling myself that, repeating it like a daily affirmation while peering in the mirror, so I can talk myself into believing it. I truly believe that she'll continue to grow into an interesting adult. But being different is fiendishly hard during adolescence.

In the past, Lizzie always found her niche. She came across a few kids who were like her. But for some reason, lately her circle of friends has dwindled to more of a line segment. She's happy at school. She wakes up cheerfully (or at least, cheerfully for a thirteen-year-old who would much rather sleep until ten AM). She loves her teachers and is challenged academically, but she hasn't found the connection with classmates she's had in the past. I wonder if her performing arts school attracts mostly extroverts. And Lizzie is not one.

As Lizzie and I sat at the table that day she'd been dumped by her friends, I listened. I reached out and grasped her hand as she talked.

"They don't know the real me. I'm fun," she said, blinking quickly to keep the tears back. "I don't feel like I can be myself, I'm all shy and quiet."

I hugged her and wished I could make things easier. I knew exactly what she meant. How many times had I felt the same way? At parties where I don't know people well, I often cling to my husband or the friend I've come with. When I try to talk in big groups, things occasionally don't come out right. I'll say something and immediately wish I could retract it, cursing myself that the words popped out in the order they did. I'm certain the person I'm speaking with thinks I'm a weirdo. So I'll say something else to clarify, which only makes it worse. I think the proper term is "a hot mess."

❋ ❋ ❋

I was that socially inept kid, the one who spoke too quietly or too loudly, sometimes with a lag time between hearing and speaking—it was a bit like a transatlantic call on an underwater cable. This earned me a reputation for being "spacey" years before I smoked my first joint. I wasn't spacey. I was just mulling things over before answering. I was that kid who had a difficult time reading other kids, the one whose social skills were less than skillful. My clothes were not stylish; I listened to the wrong music and didn't watch the right shows. I could never tame my hair into the feathered hairstyle popular with most of the other girls in junior high.

Also, I was girl-culturally illiterate. I attempted to read my classmates' actions but had a difficult time deciphering them. I played at loving shopping, clothes, and makeup, but underneath I knew I was a fraud. Eventually, I learned to

121

"THEY TOLD ME THEY NEEDED SPACE."

"pass" and to be "one of them" when I had to, but it felt like pretend, as if I were putting on a fancy dress and being someone I was not. I think I've passed along some of these traits to Lizzie.

But is being different ultimately a positive thing? Mine propelled me far from my town, where I never felt I fit in; to adventures I would not otherwise have had with people I might never have met. After college, I traveled the world, working odd jobs—an extra in a television commercial, a waitress, an apple harvester. I taught school for a year in Paris and eventually ended up in New York City, a place where I felt I belonged even before I unpacked the boxes in my walk-up tenement sublet. My people! Had I been quirk-free, would my life have played out differently? I'm sure it would have. I imagine I would have been happy regardless. I don't think that's a side effect of being different. But because I was so miserable, I didn't hesitate to leave my town and take chances elsewhere. Emotionally, I'd packed my bags years before.

※　※　※

Lizzie has little fear of new situations. She headed off to sleepaway camp at ten and has gone back each summer, reconnecting with the friends she's corresponded with all year. Last year, she went to astronomy camp for a week without knowing anyone else and easily made friends. However, those drawn there tended to be as quirky as she— introverted girls with glasses and an interest in science. Her people!

But sometimes it's hard—and I wish she had an easier time. Before going off to summer camp a few years ago, she selected a notepad with a reproduction of one of Andy Warhol's Campbell's Soup Cans on the cover. She clutched it to her chest, saying it would be perfect for writing poems, and soon began filling it with poetry. She stuffed it into her day pack for the long bus ride to camp the next morning. The following week we got a message from the counselor at camp that someone had ripped out her poems. I could feel each of those pages ripping deep inside me.

I know middle school can be the epicenter of cruel child activity, and I'm relieved that Lizzie is happy most of the time. But I hate seeing her excluded—that too-common side effect of quirkiness. I dislike seeing the shame and embarrassment in her eyes when, walking to our car after school, she says "Bye" to a classmate who doesn't answer and looks through her as if she didn't exist. There's a fine line between letting her sort it out on her own and knowing when to get involved. She tries to do the former but sometimes needs the latter. We've enlisted the middle school coordinator's help— she helps children speak to one another about how a particular word or action made them feel. Every middle school should have someone like her. We're also reassessing if her school is a good fit. As with a piece of clothing, what fits one child might hang awkwardly off another. It's a tiny school, a small pond stocked with socially suave girl fish, who are mostly dancers and performers. And Lizzie is not.

Sometimes I wish I could stash her away in a turret and buffer her from the pains of the next few years, but of course I can't. Last summer, we ran into a schoolmate and her mom at our local ice-cream place. The mom, whom I like, pulled out a chair and sat down with us. Her daughter looked visibly uncomfortable. As Lizzie and the mom chatted about British boarding schools and books (they're both fans of the Malory Towers series), her daughter glanced around to see if anyone she knew would see her. She was practically levitating from anguish, worried about her social stock—that its value would collapse like Lehman Brothers. It was as if she thought being "weird" were contagious, like the flu.

Or . . . was it my imagination? It's hard to know what rejection issues I'm bringing to the ice-cream table. There's real stuff with Lizzie, but sometimes it's hard to see through my own middle school myopia. I realize some of this is my baggage and I've got to keep it far removed from Lizzie. But it uncovers a fierce protectiveness, something deep and primal. I want to hug her and reassure her that she will find her people and that one day few of these moments will matter at all. I want to make it all better the way I did when she was little, when a kiss, a cuddle, and a Band-Aid could solve scraped knees or damaged pride.

But, through it all, I'm glad Lizzie is exactly who she is: a truly delightful child. One drizzly winter morning as we were driving to school the day after her first poem had been published by an online magazine, we were discussing her work. Now that she was not only an eighth grader but also a published writer, she had plans.

"I'm going to finish my novel. Then I'll send it out and get a million rejections. So I'll put it in a hatbox and forget about it for twenty years."

I need to add "hatbox" to the shopping list.

"You wouldn't understand."

"Try me."

Lizzie had just spent the entire day visiting a high school she was considering attending the following year and had been assigned an eleventh-grade "buddy" to show her around. Lizzie looked exactly the same as the eighth grader I'd dropped off at school that morning, dressed in her favorite jeans and layered T-shirts in contrasting (but bright) colors and her new pair of boots, but there was something slightly . . . different about her after spending the day with older kids. She had affected a new and slightly world-weary sigh.

"How'd the day go?" I asked.

"It was great. The teachers were awesome. Our English teacher is, like, funny and a good teacher, but the class was boring, because they were writing an essay." World-weary sigh. "But I got to use a computer and e-mail my friends. . . .

"The girl I shadowed said it's usually intriguing," she added, looking down at her nails, which still had a few flecks of green polish from when she'd painted them a month before.

I raised an eyebrow.

"And I went to a bistro for lunch with her and her friends—they're *eleventh* graders. I had a *grilled* chicken sandwich," she said, throwing her head back slightly.

Apparently eighth graders have chicken sandwiches while eleventh graders have *grilled* chicken sandwiches.

If this was Lizzie after one day of high school, I wondered what I should expect once she was actually going to high school.

"So what did you guys chat about?" I asked.

"Oh, stuff."

"What sort of stuff?"

"High school girl stuff."

Conversations about boys, sex, drugs, and alcohol danced through my head. Then I remembered those were my high school topics, not hers.

"Like boys?"

"Oh, you wouldn't understand," she said with yet another sigh.

"Try me," I said.

"It's a kid thing. I mean, a high school thing."

I changed the subject. I knew Lizzie really meant, "You wouldn't understand because you're old. You're not ultra-cool like the eleventh-grade girl is."

Sometimes, it takes a little bit of deciphering to translate what Lizzie says into what she means. I've often thought that it would be nice to have a guidebook for me and my fellow parents, so I've started developing one based on commonly heard phrases.

What's said ...	What's meant ...
"In a minute."	"I'll do what you're asking sometime within the next minute and this lifetime."

"I love you."	"I do love you, but I'm going to ask for a big favor. And I want you to say yes."
"I hate you!"	"I actually love you, but I'm seriously annoyed that you won't let me stay out until one AM, drive to New Orleans with a friend, or go to that party where *everyone* will be."
"Everyone else gets parents to do it."	"My friend's friend's are letting him do it. I think."
"You're so unfair!"	"I disagree with whatever it was you just told me to do or that I couldn't do."
"You're not my boss."	"Older people work. They have bosses. Bosses are in charge. Therefore, you are not in charge of me. Ha!"
"You wouldn't understand."	"You're no longer a teenager or even in your twenties, so how could I possibly expect you to grasp this important concept I'm trying to impart to you?"
"Mom, Mom, Mom . . ."	"I'm trying to get your attention in a truly annoying manner. It worked when I was two, so maybe it will work again."

"I need the computer for homework."	"I need the computer for homework. And to chat. And to go on all sorts of fun websites. And to chat some more."
"Whatever."	"That's a really stupid idea, but, like, I'll do it anyway. Only because you're making me."
"Fine."	"It's anything but fine."
"I'm not a kid anymore."	"I'm still a kid, but I want you to treat me like an adult. Except when I want a cuddle and reassurance, and then you can treat me like a kid. But never, ever, in front of any other children, because that would embarrass me."
"I promise."	"I do promise. Unless something I can't possibly foresee happens. Then, oops."
"No!"	"Another toddler word resurfaces. It means the same as it did when I was two—I'm asserting my independence, and I refuse to do whatever it is you asked. Funny how childhood comes full circle like that."

"I GOT A 3 ON MY ESSAY."

got a 3 on my Ancient Civilization essay," Lizzie said softly one
day after school when she was in
sixth grade. As always, she'd worked on this essay on her
own for several days, both in school and at home, and she'd
been certain it was marvelous.

"It happens, sweetie," I said. "Did you talk to your
teacher about what you can do differently next time?"

"I never got below a 4 before," she said. She looked as
though she might burst into tears. "Maybe I just can't do it."

Lizzie's new school issued grades on a scale of 1 to 5, and
it took her about thirty seconds to realize a 5 was an A and
a 1 was appalling. (She'd previously been in schools that
offered parents long written evaluations of their children's
progress instead of grades.) She immediately focused on ac-
quiring as many 5s as she could, riding herself like a quarter
horse to earn excellent grades. There's a downside to main-
taining such high standards for herself: if she doesn't think
she can do something perfectly the first time, she is hesitant
to attempt it for fear of not doing it correctly and risking a
poor grade.

When Lizzie started school, she took to it as if it were her natural habitat. She would spring out of bed before the alarm jolted Jeff and me awake, singing happily as she pulled on the clothes she'd chosen the previous evening to wear to kindergarten, first grade, second, then third. She'd skip into her classroom, even though each year she would be lugging the latest in a series of ever-burgeoning backpacks, which by eighth grade was probably heavier than anything an infantryman carried when he hit the beach on D-Day. She darted out of school with snippets of new songs and facts to share with us.

"We're growing chickens from eggs!" preschool Lizzie shouted, twirling around the living room.

"We sent letters to our pen pals in Ghana. That's in West Africa!" Lizzie enlightened us in fourth grade.

"Shakespeare used iambic pentameter in the play we're doing," eighth-grade Lizzie informed us.

Although through the years there have been a few social challenges (she's an introverted, slightly geeky child who develops interests in things her classmates might not find fascinating: teaching herself all about ancient Egypt in second grade, writing a musical with a friend in fourth, peppering her speech with 1940s British slang in seventh), through it all she has always thrived academically. She not only wants to learn but also loves to do so, enamored of both rules and pleasing the teacher. When she received her first ever homework assignments, she attacked them systematically, spreading out crayons and construction paper on her desk and getting to work. It was no different in later grades, except the crayons and construction paper were replaced by pens, highlighters, and college-ruled paper—when the work didn't require a computer.

I remember how Jeff and I glanced at each other when a parent expressed concern during a seventh-grade parent/teacher night: "How can I get my son to do his homework? He just won't do it."

We had other issues and questions, but this was something we'd never had to ask about. Lizzie seemed to have been born with an internal calendar, happy to schedule her work. Actually, she was born as if she'd penciled it in her agenda—she was one of the 5 percent of babies who arrive on their due date. Didn't everyone's child plan accordingly? We felt as though we'd won the parental lottery.

Like most lottery winners, though, we discovered a small downside to our great fortune. Even early on in her school career, she didn't want to make mistakes. ("I want to do it the right way.") We don't like seeing Lizzie get frustrated or upset if she can't do something perfectly right away, whether it's throwing dice for multiplication math homework in fourth grade or writing a five-paragraph essay on Kafka in sixth. And there has been quite a bit of frustration, since, face it, who completes a task perfectly the first time around? We'd love to find a way to help Lizzie regulate the pressure she puts on herself. A little bit of it is good—it helps motivate her to do a conscientious job with her work—but too much of it certainly isn't. We've been working with Lizzie and with her teachers through the years to push down this innate impulse, but it continues to spring up like a jack-in-the-box.

* * *

I understand this innate impulse because I also suffer from the all-or-none thinking common to perfectionists: "I don't get it, so why bother?" "It" can refer to anything from trigonometry, to programming my running watch, to making a chocolate mousse.

When friends visit, I've got to vacuum and mop and dust to make our house look as if it's always effortlessly spotless. When it's just our family, I'm fine living in what could objectively be called light grime. But I can't relax and enjoy friends' company if there are dust bunnies loitering under the sofa. I have to be at the airport hours before a flight. (You never can tell how long it will take to find a parking spot, clear security, or locate the gate.) If I get a rejection from an editor I've worked with in the past, I have to remind myself that it doesn't mean my writing career is over. My inborn inclination is to curl up in a fetal position on the floor in a corner of my office and rock back and forth, sobbing.

I do try to relax and take a breath before falling back into to those habits. I don't want to model this behavior, parading my tendencies in front of Lizzie so she learns that everything she does hinges on her making no mistakes and appearing flawless. When we first noticed her perfectionism, we started making instructional "mistakes" in front of her. Jeff is good at this—while playing Chutes and Ladders when Lizzie was younger, he'd say, "Oops, I landed on a slide. Oh well." As she got older, he told her stories during dinner about how, when he was in seventh grade, he was miserable at algebra, but his teacher said she would always give him a good enough grade to pass the class as long as he did his best. I try, too, but sometimes it seems like a sham as I straighten my cloth napkin and wipe up crumbs from the table.

But Lizzie also has a strong realist streak. I like to think this is Jeff's doing. Her work is always very much her own, and she doesn't seem to compare it with other children's. At the fifth-grade medieval fair, it was easy to tell Lizzie's poster board presentation was hers, with its squiggly hand-drawn titles and paper that she had researched herself. She wasn't bothered by "competing" with classmates' projects, some of which had obviously benefited from parental help; I especially recall a castle built to scale from small bricks that had been mortared together. The structure also featured a working catapult, a feat of engineering that would have been a challenge to a graduate architect. Lizzie didn't need our help to feel proud of her work.

Slowly, she's starting to realize that Western civilization won't crumble if she misses problems on a math test or gets a 3 on an essay. If we can't undo her perfectionism, we can at least lessen its effects. The ultimate goal is to raise a healthy, happy, productive, independent kid. But then again, our family places a big value on education. We have high expectations for Lizzie and want her to do well in school. How should Jeff and I balance our aspirations for her with her abilities? And is it possible to do this without adding to her perfectionist tendencies?

* * *

Since she started school, Lizzie has occasionally asked about life after high school. After her first day of preschool, we walked, hand in hand, to the playground. Lizzie sat on a green park bench, swinging her legs back and forth as she nibbled on apple slices, and we chatted about school. Lizzie wanted to know what came after preschool.

"Kindergarten," I told her.

"What's after kindergarten?" she asked.

And so it went, first, second, third grade, all the way through high school and college.

"What's after college?" Lizzie inquired.

"Grad school," I said. "If you want, anyway."

"I don't want to go to grad school!" Lizzie wailed.

I assured her she didn't have to go as other parents in the playground looked at us with a mixture of shock and amusement.

* * *

Lizzie's looking into the distance to see beyond where she is now. She seems to assume college is a fact and that she'll need it for her chosen career. Over the years, her desired careers have spanned the gamut: mommy, elf, chef, novelist, musician, songwriter, poet, science teacher, astronaut, librarian, astrochemist, astrophysicist.

Occasionally, her dad or I will ask what she plans to do for work when she's an adult. It changes, but we always nod earnestly as she announces the latest. Sometimes we'll suggest possibilities, some more realistic than others:

What about a thief? ("I don't want to go to jail.")

A surgeon? ("I don't like blood and needles.")

An electrician? ("Electricity is dangerous.")

* * *

The summer before eighth grade, Jeff took Lizzie on a "tour" of Columbia University, where he attended journalism school. Lizzie enjoyed it more than any of us had thought she would. She was awed by the library with its "millions of floors of books." At the bookstore, she bought a T-shirt with the college's name in slightly raised letters. When she wears the shirt, she rubs her fingers over them as if they're a magic lamp and she's attempting to free the genie trapped inside. The genie holding the thick envelope containing an admittance letter.

"Can I go here?" she asked, eyes wide. College is something concrete and obtainable now and not just some intangible idea flickering in the distant future.

Even though Lizzie is too young to really think about which college will fit her (and I suspect her interests and career choices will change as frequently as teen clothing styles between now and then), I think it was helpful for her to see college as a physical place and not just a mental construct. Although planning for it, with its SATs and actual campus visits, is a few years down the road, it's one we're traveling autobahn fast. It's bittersweet to see it glittering in the distance—the end of her childhood and the beginning of life on her own. Provided she can find a job after she's finished so she doesn't boomerang back home.

"MOM, I'M NOT A KID ANYMORE."

(and everything in between)

"MOM, I'M NOT A KID ANYMORE."

I recently discovered I have a superpower: I can embarrass my daughter simply by existing. This is a fairly new power that has subtly been strengthening as my daughter grows. I don't even need to don a sparkly cape or zip up a red lamé bustier, although if I did—and wore them during carpool pickup—it surely would horrify Lizzie even more (although my husband might be thrilled). I can just see my daughter covering her face with a hand and scooting down in her chair. "Mom, you're *so* embarrassing," she whispers, words I've heard so many times lately, they're almost a mantra.

Not all that many years ago, I was like a divine being to my daughter. I could do no wrong. During her toddler and preschool years, I was the all-powerful, all-knowing, benevolent deity.

"Mommy, is that right?" Lizzie would ask, and I'd nod my head, my word taken as sacrosanct.

"We can have cookies 'cause Mommy said so," she'd announce to a friend during a playdate. And that was the end of the story.

Over time, there was a slow erosion from Mom as the One to Mom as One of Many. Lizzie was learning that parents don't know it all. I encouraged this, saying, "Of course moms and dads don't know everything." In preschool, this statement was treated with shock. Now it's a given, given by her with an attempt at an eye roll. (Lizzie can do many things, but these have proved elusive. Her dad and I tell her that she's too wonderful a child to roll her eyes well.)

I suspect that when she was little and I was a single mom—and before that, the primary parent, since my first husband, because of his illness, wasn't able to be there emotionally for her—Lizzie may have put more than her share of faith in me. For the first four years of her life, I was pretty much alone in the strong spotlight of her awe, and there was no one to share it with. Later, when Lizzie was five and we moved in with Jeff, the spotlight diluted a bit, but my word was still golden, like the poster board crown she wore for her birthday party that year.

But now that she's thirteen, her four favorite words seem to be "Mom, you're so embarrassing!" If we're in public, Lizzie says it quietly. If we're in private, she'll loudly forewarn me: "Please don't embarrass me." I knew this was coming. I really did. But it still takes me a bit by surprise that the very same child who not that many years ago would pull me by the hand to proudly introduce me to new friends ("This is my mommy") now still holds my hand occasionally as we walk—but only if no one is watching. By "no one," I mean no child remotely near her age, including ones she doesn't know. If we're strolling arm in arm, she'll tighten her shoulders and pull away, as if she's cheating on other kids with a mom. Or perhaps she thinks she's too old to show affection for her parents in public. I get it and I respect it. She's both a little kid who enjoys maternal snuggles and a burgeoning young adult who wants to assert her independence. I know the next few years will be filled with more expert eye rolling and autonomy and far less cuddling. I like to think, however, that she'll eventually realize I'm nowhere near as embarrassing as she currently thinks I am. Hopefully by the time she's thirty.

We talk about all sorts of things at home and in the car—both "safe" places, devoid of other teens—but I can't bring up any "potentially embarrassing" subjects elsewhere. The catalog of embarrassing topics changes from day to day, but there are pretty consistent taboo subjects: boys, mean girls from school, and toddler pictures where she shows too much skin. (I've been forbidden from posting on Facebook an adorable photo of her on a tricycle because she fretted it showed too much leg. She was three.) In the "safe" places, her dad and I joke that we're going to whisk out a photo of her at two, prancing naked in the bathtub while clutching a purple umbrella, and tack it to her trifold display at the science fair, how we're going to tell the parents of the boy she has a crush on that we expect his intentions to be honorable, and that we're moving into a nice little apartment next to her dorm when she heads off to college. Lizzie's response is always the same: "No! No! No! Don't you dare—that would be *so* embarrassing!" Then she starts laughing. She realizes these conversations are over the top. It almost seems that when we're so ridiculous and silly, it deconstructs her embarrassment, for a moment, at least. And of course Lizzie knows we'd never, ever really do anything like this.

If I forget about the rules for a split second and bring up any potentially mortifying subject, like the name of her crush, in a public place, like the park, her discomfort is palpable. She hunches over, blanches, and says, "Mo-oooom!"

Almost as if the boy has stashed spies behind each tree, intent on catching anyone who is infatuated with him.

＊　＊　＊

Back in junior high and high school, I really did have the world's most embarrassing parents. Or at least I thought so.

I was on our town's year-round swim team. Parents were encouraged to volunteer, and mine did, writing the newsletter, stuffing their station wagon full of young teens, and driving through several nearby states to meets where they chaperoned our motel stays. But to a young me, my parents weren't just Volunteers. They were Embarrassing.

Watching my dad excitedly cheer for our relay, jumping up and down like a hyperactive kangaroo, I wished I had an Aqua-Lung and could sink to the bottom of the pool until the swim meet was over. But although I didn't appreciate him, my friends did. "Your dad's great!" Heidi, a teammate, squealed. Of course, her father often wore a beanie cap with a propeller on it. My mom, while far more subdued, worked on the newsletter, which involved interviewing my teammates. And to adolescent me, having my mom chat with my friends was just plain humiliating.

Surely no one else's parents filled their kids with such shame. No one else's parents asked really anguishing questions like "Would you like a soda?"

It's funny, though. A few days before my thirtieth high school reunion, I got together with Lori, a friend I hadn't seen in decades. At an outdoor café in the balmy New Orleans night, over oyster po'boys and Abita beer, we caught each other up on assorted parents and siblings.

"Tell your folks hi from me," Lori said. "They were always so cool."

Cool? I thought. Even thirty years after hanging up my swimsuit and my mortification for my parents from that time, this was a new descriptor. When I was young, they were kind, loving, and embarrassing—the only thing "cool" in our house was our central A/C. I asked what she meant.

"They took me to my first Jazz Fest."

Ah, the New Orleans Jazz & Heritage Festival. I remember the time my friend was referring to. We were fifteen and we huddled together in the backseat of my parents' gray Toyota Corona, begging that they switch the radio to a station that specialized in stadium rock, performed by men in spandex outfits and long, wavy hair. My mom pressed the preset button. Country music gave way to something like REO Speedwagon. My musical taste from my youth leaves my adult palate ashamed—I truly didn't deserve Jazz Fest. At the festival, after agreeing where and when to meet, we fled. And then we reveled, drinking beer from large plastic cups and swaying to the Radiators and Muddy Waters, enjoying the "jazz" and "heritage" aspects of the day, although we were far more interested in the "festive."

Several hours later we rode back home, tipsy, with my parents. I'm sure they were unaware of our activities, although I suspect we must have smelled a bit like the Dixie brewery. This didn't really make them "cool"—just blissfully oblivious. Or did they notice but not say anything? But then again, if they had asked about our exploits, my friend and I would have admitted nothing and denied everything.

Near the end of seventh grade, I chauffeured Lizzie and her friend to a dance performance.

They seemed acutely aware an adult was in the car.

"What did you think of Speech and Debate today?" Sadie asked.

"It was okay," Lizzie answered after glancing at me.

They both were sitting up very straight. I don't recall Lizzie ever having such perfect posture.

I maneuvered the car into a parking spot outside a pizzeria. They huddled near each other and walked into the restaurant, choosing a table near the door. As if they hoped to make a quick getaway from me.

"Thank you so much for dinner," Sadie said, picking up a plastic menu from the table.

"My pleasure," I told her, and was greeted with an awkward silence.

"May I please have a soda tonight?" Lizzie asked.

"Of course," I answered, to another silence.

They were awfully polite.

"Hey, guys, I need to get some work done. I'll sit over here," I said, pointing to a Formica table across the restaurant. I sat and pretended to be engrossed in a pile of work. They probably would have been happier if I were sitting in an entirely different pizza restaurant, one down the street or across town. While I edited a paper, the timbre of their conversation immediately changed, though I couldn't make out any actual words. They became both more relaxed and animated and shed the parent-polite kidskins from minutes before. From my perch across the room, I strove to morph into a new superhero, Boring Mother.

I must have succeeded, because later Lizzie thanked me.

"WHAT KIND OF QUESTION IS THIS?"

Lizzie watched from the doorway as I blotted my lipstick in the bathroom mirror, readying myself for a date with Jeff.

"Are you going to a romantic restaurant and stare lovingly into each other's eyes while you sip tea?" Lizzie asked.

At thirteen, Lizzie's idea of dating—the grown-up version, at least—is welded together from Jane Austen and the Betsy-Tacy books she's been scooping up in secondhand bookstores. Some young teens like vintage couture; she likes vintage books.

Lizzie seems younger than many of her middle school classmates. And frankly, I'm thrilled. Some of her classmates watch R-rated movies. Some are dating. Lizzie told us about a few "couples" in her seventh-grade class, although she wasn't quite sure what this entailed other than changing Facebook statuses and announcing to other children that they were dating. Lizzie is in a different place, with both feet still planted firmly in childhood, only an occasional toe dunked into teen issues. She still enjoys playing games of hide-and-seek with a neighborhood friend and much prefers seeing a movie at the mall to shopping or hanging out there.

Lizzie had a crush on a boy last year, whose name I've been sworn never to reveal. This crush was her first "real" one, involving analyzing him with friends and, once or twice, speaking with the actual boy. She developed an earlier infatuation in fourth grade. We knew, not because she ever said anything, but because she taped her class list to the back of her door and there, next to a boy's name, was a carefully drawn heart, inked in purple marker.

Not long ago, Lizzie and I went to the pediatrician's office for her thirteen-year-old well-child visit. She fidgeted as she sat on the examination table, crinkling the paper under her. She was concerned about the HPV shot she would receive. She'd heard it was painful.

"I know what it's for. My friends told me," she announced, twisting the paper nervously.

I asked what.

She leaned in closer, to the edge of the table, put her hand in front of her mouth, and whispered, "Sex."

I confirmed that, yes, it's a vaccination to help prevent cervical cancer that can be caused by a virus that's spread during sex. And it's most effective to give the shots now, when girls are kids and before they become much older and have sex. (In my mind I added, "Much, much, much older.")

Lizzie and I had already had the "sex talk" the previous year, and on the shelf in her room she keeps the same book I'd bought for our talk. Occasionally, I see her flopped on her leopard-print beanbag chair, studying it. As questions have come up, she seems comfortable asking me. I answer all her questions in a matter-of-fact manner and hope that she'll continue to ask me anything that pops into her head, although I know this could change as she gets older. When

I was growing up, "sex" of all kinds was pretty much a four-letter word, if it was uttered by adults at all.

After Lizzie was weighed and measured, blood pressure checked, the nurse handed her a clipboard. During previous visits, we'd received a form that parents filled out, but now that Lizzie was a teen, she got to fill one out herself. I asked Lizzie if she wanted privacy.

"No, Mom, stay," she said, voice quivering. The pen shook in her hand as she wrote. Lizzie does not like the doctor's office. Especially when needles are involved.

She read questions and scribbled answers. Then she paused.

"What kind of question is this?" she sputtered. I asked if she wanted to tell me what it was.

"They want to know if I'm interested in boys or girls. That's private!" she said.

Lizzie's indignation didn't stem from homophobia. She's grown up seeing many different kinds of families. It's a non-event that her friend Charlie has two moms or Austin has two dads. There are straight couples, gay couples, single straight mothers, single gay mothers, single gay and straight fathers. All of them, to Lizzie and her friends, are simply "parents." (Therefore, inherently embarrassing.) Lizzie's issue with the question was that it was *her* business whom she liked—boys or girls—rather than the doctor's. I told her the form was for kids her age as well as older teens—and some a bit older might have questions about sex that the doctor could answer if they didn't feel comfortable asking their parents.

After Lizzie's doctor's appointment, we got into the car to drive home. As I fastened my seat belt, I looked over at Lizzie and asked, "I know some of the girls in your class are going out with boys—are any gay and lesbian kids dating, too?"

"No, I don't think so," Lizzie said, rummaging through the glove compartment for her favorite CD.

Maybe, even in a progressive school in a progressive city, middle schoolers could be unsure about their sexuality or uncomfortable about being viewed as "different." I've seen same-sex couples holding hands near the local high schools, so perhaps it's the age—they're sorting it out and discovering who they are.

As of now, anyway, Lizzie seems to have self-identified as "straight." If she self-identified otherwise, it would be a non-issue in our house and in our community.

* * *

When I went to high school, no one was out of the closet. Our town was situated deep in the Bible Belt, and I don't remember seeing any same-sex couples pushing shopping carts through the aisles of the local Winn-Dixie. There were gay people, but they lived in New Orleans and were often called something else by some of our town's citizens, nouns that generally began with "q" or "f."

This was decades before the It Gets Better campaign, and I suspect it really didn't for gay youth in my small conservative town in the early eighties. A boy wearing a pink button-up shirt was "preppy"—but a boy who had hair a bit longer than what was considered normal was "faggy."

One of the boys I smoked pot with when I was in eleventh grade was a fine-featured wispy teen with blue eyes and a quiet demeanor. Some of the jocks gave him a hard time in school since he favored black Led Zeppelin T-shirts and his hair was halfway down his back. A few years later, home on a visit from college, I heard from a friend that one night his car had run out of gas and he attempted to hitchhike to a service station. A car stopped. A door opened. He jumped in. The men who picked him up called him "fag" while they beat him so badly that he ended up in the hospital. Thankfully, he was okay—at least physically. A year or so after the incident, I saw him working in a local store. We said hello and briefly caught each other up on our lives. He didn't say anything about being beaten and I didn't ask about it.

In our high school, differences were not discussed or accepted by teens or teachers. During a poetry unit in tenth-grade English class, the teacher called on various students to read aloud from the book. One poem we read contained the word *gay*. A few students snickered. The teacher angrily told them to stop.

"I remember when 'gay' was a happy word. Now . . . ," she said, shaking her head sadly.

If there were any gay children in our class, I can't imagine what they were thinking.

I knew that I was "straight" by middle school. Although if I hadn't been, I'm not sure I would have known otherwise. Erin, a friend from high school, recently told me that she didn't know she was a lesbian until she was in her twenties. When she was thirteen, her older sister sat her down and told her that their parents were concerned she might be having "different feelings" and that it wasn't okay. Because she was frightened of losing her family's love, Erin repressed her real self for many years.

In eighth grade I developed my first crush, falling for an older man: Andy Gibb. As I stared at the *Tiger Beat* centerfold I'd taped to my wall, I sighed. I shadow danced in my room with him and I practiced kissing his lips, although they were as stiff and cold as the paper they were printed on. When a friend from swim team came over, we gazed at Andy. He stared vacantly back at us.

Back then, before either of us had actually kissed a boy, we spent a lot of time and energy on the subject, examining its various aspects and techniques thoroughly. We took turns standing in a corner of my room, our backs toward each other, hands crisscrossed and wrapped around our front side so it appeared that we were locked in an amorous embrace with an actual person. I pretended this was Andy Gibb. We added sound effects for good measure—"Oh, oh, oh!"—and lots of lip-smacking noises.

Around this time, I developed my first crush on a genuine boy, although I didn't tell anyone who he was. I would simply stare at him and picture our life together. We'd hold hands! We'd go to PG movies! We'd move into a little house after high school and . . . do whatever it was that grown-ups did in their little houses. Eat fondue and no-bake cheese-cake! A few years ago, I looked him up on Facebook and learned that although he's still cute, he is very interested in football, posting about it a lot. He also seems to enjoy making extremist right-wing rants, often with multiple spelling and grammar errors. Even if I had announced my crush on him back in junior high, it never would have worked out. What on earth had I been thinking back then? We had nothing in common!

One day in high school, after my first boyfriend and I had been dating a few months, we drove to his friend Dan's house. Although my boyfriend was a pot smoker, this friend was a football player. My boyfriend was one of those rare kids who could move freely among different peer groups. To almost everyone else, traveling from one clique to another was a bit like traveling to Communist Russia. It involved visas and a local tour guide. For example, even though I made good grades, since I was a member of the Potheads I wasn't about to waltz over to the Smart Kids and discuss Dante. Nor could I cancan over to the Popular Girls, the circle of gorgeous cheerleaders and dance team girls, and discuss whatever it was popular girls talked about. There were few (if any) defections from cliques. It seemed once you pledged allegiance to one, you were in it for life. Or at least until graduation. But my boyfriend was a free agent.

One afternoon we sat in the living room of my boyfriend's football player friend, talking about muscle cars and deer hunting. My boyfriend asked Dan how things were going with his long-term girlfriend. Dan leaned in.

"Great! We did it," he said. "But you can't tell *anyone*. I don't want her to get a reputation."

This was the state of sex in my high school. Boys were encouraged by other boys to have it, but girls couldn't, or their character was besmirched if word got out that they'd "done it." Dan wanted to keep his girlfriend safe from this. He didn't want to chance that she would be called a "slut." And other children who had "different feelings" couldn't or didn't express them. Intolerance and repression were the facts of life.

Lizzie is growing up in a home and at a time where sex and sexual identity are discussed. She is accepted for who she is and not for what others think she should or shouldn't do or be. Whatever her dating future holds in store, I can pretty much bet intolerance and repression won't be part of it. Who knows what lies ahead in the coming years? Maybe even something involving a romantic restaurant and staring lovingly into someone's eyes while sipping tea.

"PLEASE, PLEASE CAN WE GO?"

The station wagon carrying Lizzie and her friends home from school could have been powered by their excited chatter. At least that's how it seemed to me from the vantage point of the front porch swing. As they pulled into the driveway, Lizzie hopped out, barely able to contain herself.

"Mom, Rick Riordan is going to sign books tonight. Can we go—please?"

The mom who was driving leaned out the window.

"Sorry," she called out sheepishly. "Maybe I shouldn't have said anything."

Portland, where we had moved a couple months earlier, is home to Powell's Books, which is arguably the world's best bookstore. Taking up an entire city block, with a few satellite shops in nearby neighborhoods, it's the type of place that doesn't just sell books; it celebrates them. It attracts all sorts of writers, almost as if it's a migratory stop for flocks of authors traversing the country. Portlanders also seem to hold authors in high esteem, so Lizzie's devotion to Riordan fit right in. This was one of her favorite authors at her favorite bookstore. We didn't have any plans for the evening and she'd already finished her homework during study hall, so how could we not go?

Lizzie is a book lover. A mention of Riordan or Suzanne Collins makes Lizzie giddy with delight. Lizzie is the kind of kid who lingers in libraries for fun and whose idea of a really great evening is her monthly book club meeting, where she gets to chat with like-minded tweens and teens about how excellent *The Book Thief* is.

She was an avid reader even before she could read. She started with black-and-white graphic–filled board books, but her favorite was one that contained photos of babies' faces, which she doused with slobbery kisses. That the book was well chewed was, as I occasionally boast, proof that even early on she literally hungered for literature.

As a toddler, she danced and swayed as I singsonged the poetry of *Chicka Chicka Boom Boom*, losing herself in the melody. At our local library, she'd sit on the floor with one book in her lap and twenty piled next to her, turning pages and reading pictures.

Well into the upper reaches of elementary school, her dad and I read to her each night. In second grade, Lizzie became enthralled by the Bobbsey Twins, which Jeff read to her. Mostly to amuse himself, however, he took artistic liberties and the stories regularly swerved in a slightly warped direction, as sweet little Flossie, the youngest twin, would meet an unfortunate end every night. She was flattened like a pancake under a steamroller, lost to the heavens in a runaway hot-air balloon, and eaten by bloodthirsty sharks. Lizzie was less horrified by Flossie's nightly grisly demise than she was by Jeff's deviations from the text.

"Jeff, read it the way it is!" Lizzie demanded in a fit of giggles.

Those reading-aloud sessions are more than cherished memories. They were one of the most important ways Lizzie learned to love books. Of course, with two parents who write for a living and a house stuffed with well-worn paperbacks and hardcovers, I suppose it wasn't a complete surprise. Lizzie often saw us sprawled on the sofa, engrossed in our books, and it was natural for her to want to join us.

Her love of reading isn't without issue, though. It sometimes seems that she favors the company of books over that of other children. Although we appreciate that Lizzie loves literature, reading is by nature a solitary pursuit. It's not as if she's going to have a new friend over to her house and they'll sit, side by side, reading. (Although this does happen with a few bookish buddies she knows well.) And Lizzie will bring whatever she's reading at the moment on even short car trips, preferring printed words to the spoken. (Or those uttered by her parents, anyway.) So we worry—is her love of literature making her antisocial? I imagine the same dilemma is faced by other parents whose child is so captivated by one activity that it seems it's almost at the expense of others, whether the favored pastime is Xbox or gymnastics. How can parents help a child balance the love of a particular pursuit with other interests? We certainly want to continue to encourage Lizzie's appreciation of reading, but we don't want it to preclude other social activities.

* * *

That night, as we got into the car, Lizzie gripped her copy of Riordan's *The Red Pyramid*, which she'd bought the day it was released. She bent over the book and kissed it.

Even though we got to the bookstore early, an impressive five hundred children had arrived before us. I know this because almost all the free tickets for the event had been given out and Lizzie snagged one of the few remaining. The kids chattered excitedly but softly. Most were clutching books to their chests and impatiently waiting in line to meet the author. None of them, though, kissed their books.

How great that all these children wanted to meet the person whose writing had taken them places—in their imaginations, and then to that very bookstore. Events like these sometimes make me wonder whether we're encouraging reading or hero worship. But kids need heroes, and I'd much rather Lizzie's be someone who writes books than someone whose claim to fame is their looks.

* * *

When I was a sixth grader, I loved Enid Blyton's books and Hergé's Tintin series but never felt the connection to the authors that Lizzie seems to have found. Possibly because Blyton was dead and Hergé was from Belgium, which was a mysterious country far away from Indonesia, where we then lived. In Jakarta, English-language books were difficult to find, but every six months we flew to Singapore for vaccinations, dental work, and an English-language bookstore, where we stocked up on reading material for the following six months. In Indonesia we had no television, so books and the Voice of America on shortwave radio were our only forms of in-home media entertainment.

The following year, when we moved back to the States, I still read, but not as voraciously. We now had a television, which I watched daily. And it wasn't all that easy to find books for young teens. I'm not even sure our library had a young adult section, and I felt far too old and worldly for children's books. In eighth grade, a neighborhood girl gave me a copy of Judy Blume's *Forever. . .*, which I read clandestinely and cluelessly. Because it's about a girl losing her virginity and I'd never had the talk about sex with my mom, I was kind of an idiot about the book's subject matter. I did, however, understand what the boy's "Ralph" was. A few years later, I discovered that my first boyfriend had given his penis a moniker, too ("Charlie"). Even at sixteen, I found there was something a bit off-putting about giving one's sex organ a name.

When I asked my parents for book recommendations, my dad handed me a paperback copy of *In Cold Blood*. I read it in bed over a week. Each night I had sweating nightmares that a couple of psychopaths would drive through the streets of our small town, make a left into our subdivision and a right into our cul-de-sac, and somehow find our small ranch-style brick house.

It never would have occurred to me as a young teen to go and hear an author read. If either Judy Blume or Truman Capote were to have visited a bookstore in my town (highly unlikely since our town didn't have a bookstore; we had to drive to New Orleans for one), I doubt I would have gone to see them, clutching their books to my chest and jumping up and down with excitement along with fellow readers. Plus, Judy Blume probably would have been run out of our conservative town, blamed for corrupting its youth.

It wasn't until right after college that I fell in love with books permanently, stronger and more forcefully than before. All through high school and part of college, I'd felt a little lost: lost about who I was, lost in a haze of marijuana smoke, lost finding reading material. But after college, I finally had the time and the curiosity to explore on my own. During a yearlong trip through Australia and the South Pacific, there were large chunks of free time, and since I didn't have much money for entertainment, I read. I traded books with other backpackers (cringing if I got stuck with a Sidney Sheldon book for the eighteen-hour freighter trip from Raratonga to Aitutaki). But mostly I discovered writers I liked, ones I'd earlier ignored or been ignorant of in high school when we didn't read complete novels in English class.

* * *

Lizzie is the type of reader I wish I'd been when I was her age. She actually looks through the *New York Times Book Review* for kids' books and is disappointed the weeks that they're not critiqued. Her favorite librarian lives across the street, and Lizzie asks her for recommendations. She takes chances with books, trying on a variety of authors and feeling no guilt about discarding them if they're not for her.

Jeff and I have tried to help her balance her love of books with other activities, though. We've banished reading during short car trips around town—instead, we talk. She's also found more social ways to be involved with books than just participating in her monthly book group. She volunteers at the library for the summer reading program, encouraging younger readers to find books that they love. During the school year, she and a classmate helped with an organization that donates books to families in need. And Lizzie is branching out and trying new activities, like photography and tap dancing, that have nothing to do with books.

Lizzie has also had to learn, however, that not all middle schoolers share her interests—she's finding that it doesn't necessarily go over well to prattle on excitedly about Harry Potter to a classmate who is uninterested or a nonreader. She's finding her niche, though, among those who find Hermione more or less as interesting as she does.

She's also enamored of words and plays with them as if they were Legos, writing poetry and songs for her piano and filling her notebook with ideas. Right now, her highest form of praise is to announce, "Wow, that's so creative." So if she's a bit of a book groupie and wants to stand around for a few hours with five hundred other children waiting for a well-loved author, I'll happily drive her to the bookstore. And then flee to the adult section, where it's quiet enough to get some reading done.

> **"How was your trip to Mount St. Helens?"**

> **"It was, like, awesome!"**

I had just picked Lizzie up from her eighth-grade retreat, where her class had spent three days bonding and doing hands-on science activities. As she hoisted her duffel bag over her shoulder and handed me her sleeping bag, I hugged her and asked how the trip had gone.

"Mount St. Helens was, like, awesome!" she announced.

I asked why she thought so.

"It was, like, so much more awesome than our seventh-grade retreat. We had, like, more time to hang out. We, like, waded in a freezing cold lake. And then we, like, stayed up until *midnight* talking. It was so awesome. And we, like, went hiking in the ape caves because those are, like, made from lava and we were, like, studying geology. It was, like, the most awesome trip ever!"

And, like, my head hurt from hearing that dreaded word over and over.

Lately, the L-word hasn't just been seeping into Lizzie's speech; it's been slamming into it at g-force. In the past, "like" trickled into her language, but now it prefaces many of her clauses, both main and subordinate. It seems there's no grammatical reason for the word's placement: it's almost as if it's just randomly chucked into sentences. Jeff and I are fascinated by how many times she manages to cram this one small word into even a short conversation. There are other, much loved words.

"Awesome" is also used with reckless abandon. It can describe a fun activity, like the "awesome scavenger hunt" she participated in with the middle school or a tasty glass of lemonade rather than items or events that truly inspire awe. I realize this word spread to the general public years ago, but our household had been a linguistic holdout, an "awesome"-free zone. Last summer, we tried to illustrate the word's actual meaning as we hiked through the genuinely awesome redwood forest. It did not take.

"These trees are awesome!" Lizzie said as we stared up at them.

Jeff and I were pleased. Lizzie understood!

"This hotel is awesome," Lizzie commented an hour later as we checked into a 1950s motel whose interior decorator seemed to have favored a kitsch-inspired motif. The motel was across the highway from a truly awe-inspiring tourist trap. Lizzie declared both the giant carved Paul Bunyan statue and his ox to be, in her words, "awesome."

＊ ＊ ＊

"Hilarious" means something might be moderately amusing. A joke among eighth graders is hilarious.

"Epic" has absolutely nothing to do with the *Iliad* or *Odyssey*; an "epic cookie" is simply a tasty baked good.

It's as if language has suffered from definition inflation. Why have a joke be simply amusing if it can be hilarious? Why have a class trip be fun if it can be awesome?

I know that young teens find slang a way to connect with

others—it's the lingua franca of adolescence. (And way, way beyond—I hear my peers frequently use these words.) I don't want to necessarily purge Lizzie of slang in a jargon junta. Instead, Jeff and I want her to be slang-bilingual: to use it with her friends but not have it become ingrained in her everyday speech. I hope she will be able to turn it on and off at will, as if it were a spigot. Because right now, I'm not sure that she would be able to stop herself once the "likes" start flowing. If Lizzie were, say, interviewing for college today, her interview might sound a little like this:

> **Interviewer:** Tell us what you'd like to study. What inspired your interest in this subject?
>
> **Lizzie:** I'm interested in, like, astrochemistry. It's, like, awesome. A few years ago when I was, like, about to start eighth grade, I attended this totally awesome astronomy camp. We, like, learned so much about space and, like, the universe and, like, black holes and stuff that I became, like, inspired to study it more thoroughly at an awesome college. I also find, like, astrophysics compelling. Atomic particles are, like, so small. It would be so totally awesome to study this stuff because I'm, like, into it. It's hilarious that people think Earth is the center of the, like, universe when there's, like, totally so much else out there that we haven't, like, yet discovered.

Luckily, we've got a few years to help her learn when it's appropriate to use slang. Right now, most of the time we just let it go. Sometimes, though, when the "likes" are flying out of her mouth too frequently, Jeff and I will join in the conversation:

Lizzie: Oh my gosh, we had, like, the best time in theater today.

Sue: Like, what did you do?

Jeff: Was it, like, awesome?

Lizzie: We, like, played fun theater games that were, like, amazing.

Jeff: How'd you, like, play them?

Lizzie: Why are you speaking like that?

Sue: Like, what do you mean?

Lizzie: Argh! Stop! I get it!

And it seems to work. For, like, a minute or two.

"WHAT DID HE SAY?"

Our family was driving from New York's Hudson Valley to our new home in Portland, Oregon, and had stopped in Rapid City, South Dakota, after spending the day admiring the jaw-dropping rugged beauty of the Badlands and visiting what Lizzie, then eleven, called the "big heads" of Mt. Rushmore. Now we were tired and hungry and hot, since a heat wave had washed over the Great Plains. We checked into a hotel on the outskirts, rinsed our faces to cool off and freshen up, and drove downtown to find a place to eat.

We parked and strolled down Rapid City's wide and semideserted streets, searching for a restaurant. Life-size bronze statues of past presidents stood on street corners, like patriotic streetwalkers. Lizzie dashed ahead of us, hanging on president after president, wrapping her arms around them. I looked over at Jeff and grinned. He reached for my hand and squeezed gently. Louis the Dog trotted along beside us, happy to be out of the car. Flag-covered banners, hanging from corner posts, read: EXPERIENCE THE REAL AMERICA. We felt so lucky Lizzie was getting a chance to see so much of it during our cross-country drive.

But then we passed a bar in the center of town. A few outdoor tables were filled, including one covered with pitchers of beer, some of which were rapidly being depleted by three rough-looking men and a woman. They looked at us.

"If I wanted to be an asshole, I'd put on a yarmulke!" the biggest one announced, his stringy hair shaking as he laughed, pitcher in his hand. Their female acquaintance snickered and slapped her thigh.

"Chicken dance!" shouted another, and they all started clucking, flapping their arms like crazed birds, and humming a tune I recognized from countless bar and bat mitzvahs.

Jeff and I looked at each other, not fully comprehending. We whispered to each other on the way to the restaurant. Had we really heard them correctly? Surely not, right? They had to be talking about something else—perhaps we'd taken a conversation about poultry out of context. I told Jeff I thought those comments were directed at us. He said he thought I'd misheard—or hoped I had. He looked unsure. I'd never experienced anti-Semitism before. But Jeff is Jewish and was familiar with being on the receiving end of prejudiced comments. Lizzie wanted to know what we were discussing. I said we thought we heard some people say something that made us a little upset, but we weren't entirely certain.

"What did you think they said?" she asked. I told her I wasn't positive, so I didn't want to jump to conclusions, that I'd probably just misheard. Lizzie walked quietly beside us. If we had actually heard what we thought we'd heard, what would we say to Lizzie?

I'd never thought of my husband as anything other than handsome, with his silver curly hair and delft-blue eyes, but apparently he was "Jewish-looking" to these people. When I started dating, I looked for certain qualities in a man:

kind, smart, funny, and interesting. Religion wasn't even on my checklist, and since neither Jeff nor I practice one, it had never been an issue.

Lured by the scent of sizzling garlic, we found a café and sat at an outside table, our dog nestled at Jeff's feet. Two women suddenly got up from the table next to ours and moved inside. For the first time on our trip, we began to feel out of place and, frankly, a little paranoid. Did they not like the looks of us? Or were they simply too hot? Our waitress disappeared for long periods, reappearing to assist the table next to ours and seeming to ignore us. Jeff joked that it was because he was Jewish, but there was an edge to the way he said it. This had never been an issue in New York, but he was clearly a minority here, and suddenly we understood what it must feel like to others who were religious or ethnic outsiders. What had once been a comfortable and fun trip suddenly had an insidious undercurrent with a riptide of threat. Our Prius, with its New York license plates and peace sign magnet on the gas tank cover, Jeff's gorgeously fuzzy hair—these suddenly seemed like beacons, spotlighting our differences to these bigots and others like them.

After dinner, Jeff suggested we walk by the bar, just to see if we'd heard correctly. We wanted to believe that we hadn't. I was a bit afraid and argued against it, but Jeff was determined to find out. Lizzie, oblivious to our conversation and full of chocolate ice cream, ran ahead to find more president statues. So, sun low in the sky, but with enough people on the streets that it didn't feel deserted or threatening, we retraced our steps to our car, passing the bar. Sure enough, the foursome was still there; the empty beer pitchers had multiplied in the hour or so we'd been at dinner. There were other patrons at the bar as well.

"Your hair is too long for South Dakota!" the youngest

skinhead hollered. Jeff's hair wasn't long. Because it was curly, it grew out, not down.

"That's one ugly Jew dog," said a skinny man in his thirties, with long greasy hair and heavily tattooed arms. I looked at our corgi–Australian shepherd mix, puzzled. If Louis the Dog had a belief system, it was one that involved a soft bed and the neighbor's unsecured compost pile.

Jeff turned to me. "You were right." He gave me a look of shock, disappointment, and disbelief melding together. Jeff just stared at them and we walked away, not wanting to chance placing ourselves in any danger.

Normally, I like to be right, but this was one time I had really wanted to be wrong. And how to reconcile that these people felt comfortable enough voicing their opinion in the middle of the city during what passed for rush hour in Rapid City, South Dakota's second-largest city? We got into our car and locked the doors, and Jeff pointedly drove past them one more time, this time with a middle finger extended.

"Stop it," I hissed. I was scared.

"What's going on?" Lizzie demanded. She looked back at the skinheads and then at us.

How do you explain hatred and this level of ignorance to a kid? This was a question we found ourselves unprepared to answer. It had honestly never occurred to me that we'd face people like this.

At some point, kids will most likely overhear bigoted speech—or perhaps be on its receiving end. What should they do? What should a parent say to them? Jeff and I tried to explain the skinheads to Lizzie, but we felt almost at a loss to describe what could make people so hate-filled.

"Sweetie, some people blame others when their lives are maybe not what they want them to be. And they blame everyone in a group for it—it's called scapegoating," I said.

"I've read about that," Lizzie answered.

"Have you heard of anti-Semitism?" Jeff asked.

"Is it like the bad guys in the Anne Frank book?" Lizzie asked.

Yes, we said, it was. Although the situation here wasn't that extreme, we didn't know these people and were unsure if their words were just words or could turn into action, if given the chance, on a dark street. For the first time during our trip, I felt unsafe.

I also felt as if Lizzie had begun the day believing in the goodness of people and had a little of that innocence scraped away. Sooner or later, of course, it's important she realize that there are nasty people (and some dangerously so) out there— she already knows this through reading books and stories in the newspaper. But reading about intolerant people and having them direct hate at you are two very different things. I felt helpless that I couldn't protect her from others' hostility. I know that there's a difference between ignorance and hate and that those who are the first don't always do the second, but toss the two together and its alchemy is scary.

* * *

The summer after I finished fourth grade, we visited my grandparents in Missouri. My grandfather collected us from the Kansas City Airport for the long drive to the small town where my mother had grown up and where my grandparents still lived. On the highway, my grandfather beeped the horn of his American-built sedan and hollered about "the goddamn niggers," who were apparently driving either too quickly or too slowly for his liking. I was shocked to hear someone—a grown-up!—say these words I knew were bad and appalled that my parents said nothing to him about it. (I wasn't shocked by the cursing. "Well, hell . . . ," was my grandfather's standard sentence opener: "Well, hell, it sure is good to see you. Well, hell, would you like some sody pop?") My parents had no problem calling me out if I called my younger sister something like "stupid jerk." And that was nothing. But standing silently by while someone makes an ignorant and hateful comment is really pretty much the same thing as tacitly condoning it—or it appears that way to a child. I stayed silent, too.

There were other times that hateful language was thrown about like a dodgeball, either lobbed at someone to cause pain or casually tossed in the air without regard to where it would land. During junior high and high school in my small southern town, the word "fag" was a much used slur, both directed at children perceived to be gay (ones who had traits that were considered at the time to be so, anyway: a boy with a lisp or a girl who cared more about sports than clothing) and used as an adjective in a "joking" manner to describe, say, a boy's unfortunate clothing choice. Then there was the girl on my swim team who said, quietly and out of the blue before practice one day, "I don't like niggers." It wasn't so much that this was her opinion—there were plenty of silent racists in town—it was that she'd crossed an unspoken line and that she assumed we were a receptive audience. No one said anything. No one challenged her. We just changed the subject, wondering how hard Coach Kelly would work us that afternoon.

* * *

Until the South Dakota skinheads, I felt that Lizzie had been fairly sheltered. I don't think she realized there were still people who hated others just for how they look or what they believe. I think she assumed that people like that were relegated to the historical novels she liked to read or, perhaps, far-off lands. I know that as she gets older, she'll hear other racist or bigoted language. If she knows the person using the language, I wonder if she'll be brave enough to say something or if she'll sit silently by as I did. I like to imagine that she'll speak up. But if she comes across someone as hate-filled as skinheads, I hope she'll simply walk away—and then do something about it later. We drove away from the South Dakota skinheads that night, but when we got back to the hotel, Jeff wrote a letter to the local paper about the incident. It was published and opened a dialogue—one that I hope continues.

My family and I were passing through Rapid City recently on our way to Oregon.

We were charmed by how friendly everyone was as we walked around the downtown area, until we passed by a bar and some patrons sitting out front uttered several anti-Semitic comments directed at me.

Then, to make sure we understood, they were even more threatening when we passed them by later in the evening.

What a shame—in part because after being subjected to that, you can't help but wonder if everyone who looks at you a certain way feels similarly.

We also had to explain the concept of hatred to my 11-year-old who heard everything. I can't tell you how upset she was.

JEFF KISSELOFF
Portland, Oregon

Several people wrote to say that they were sorry about what happened. One said that our family should be offered a sincere apology and that such comments were inexcusable. He (or she) hoped that the rest of our visit was pleasant enough to balance out this incident.

The rest of our visit was.

"TELEPHONE FOR YOU, LIZZIE."

"Mike really wants to see Lizzie," my former mother-in-law says. She's calling to arrange a visit with my ten-year-old daughter. She and I have a warm relationship, but something in her voice catches. From the change in her tone, it's obvious she's uncomfortable in her role as visitation procuress. It's been more than a year since Mike has last seen his daughter—a year where he's been in and out of hospitals and on and off the meds that, when taken, tame his severe case of bipolar disorder.

The last time we saw him, it didn't go well. Lizzie was almost nine, and we met him and his mother for lunch. I drove us to a Thai restaurant in a scruffy upstate New York town. As we greeted each other, my daughter clung to me. In the past year, Mike had gained a lot of weight. Buttons strained against his black shirt, and his neatly trimmed beard was flecked with gray. Nervously, my daughter grabbed the back of the chair next to mine and scraped it across the polished hardwood floor, ready to crawl into it.

"Why don't you sit next to Daddy?" her grandmother suggested, getting up and motioning to Lizzie to take the seat next to Mike. Lizzie, resisting her innate desire to please other people, ignored her and stayed next to me. I smiled reassuringly at her, reached out, and rubbed her back, feeling her shoulder blades tense through the wool of her sweater, and bit the insides of my cheeks to keep the words I wanted to scream inside my mouth: "Let her decide what to call him and where to sit." I kept quiet and Lizzie stayed where she was. Before the pad thai arrived, Lizzie asked me to take her to the bathroom twice. She went six times before lunch was over. Her father left the table as often to go outside to smoke.

After settling into his chair following a cigarette break, in a voice some people use with very young children to point out kittens or fire trucks, he said to Lizzie, "I saw James Gandolfini the other day." I explained that she had no idea who that was. Then I changed the subject to how Lizzie enjoyed playing the piano and writing her own songs. Lizzie joined in and proudly announced that her piano teacher had helped her record one. "You'll have to give me your CD to give to my rock star friend. He used to play for Phish," Mike said. Lizzie stared into the distance, blankly.

"Mike, Lizzie doesn't know who that is," his mother informed him gently. I kept silent, praying for lunch to end and with it my daughter's obvious discomfort.

* * *

I hate these meetings. I know it's what a good parent must do, but it's difficult to do with a mentally ill ex. I spent the final five years of our marriage—including Lizzie's infancy—trying desperately to make him take his meds that kept him from traipsing nonstop around our apartment, awake for days, and then buying $200 shirts on our thrift-shop budget.

When Lizzie turned three, I realized he wasn't going to stay on the drugs. One night, after pacing the house for days like a caged polar bear in the zoo, he left without a word, leaving our front door unlocked behind him. I didn't know where he was or when he'd be back. As Lizzie slept, I got up and turned the dead bolt. I stayed up, waiting for him, but eventually gave up and fell asleep. Sometime before it was light, I heard the front door open and bang shut. I blinked as he turned on the kitchen lights and opened cabinet doors and kitchen drawers, slamming them. Whispering, I reminded him Lizzie was asleep and asked where he'd been. He looked at me, pupils huge, and said loudly, "I took a stroll. But I'm fine." Lizzie fussed and I got up and went into her room, holding her in the twin bed until she fell asleep. I somehow did, too. In the morning, I discovered Mike had riffled through my old family photos and turned many upside down. When I asked why he'd done it, he said calmly that he knew my relative was in the CIA and then suggested my parents should sleep in the backyard when they came to visit the following week, adding, "We could pitch a tent." I was scared.

I took my daughter and left. But I was determined to be a good parent and to make sure Lizzie had a loving relationship with her father, even if he was sick. Mike was hospitalized for a time, and after he was released and stable, we decided to meet. He came with his parents to our Brooklyn apartment for dinner. Waiting for the doorbell to ring, I fought down my worry about how he'd be with our daughter. I wanted Lizzie to have an idyllic childhood, one filled with happy memories of a mom and dad who loved her so much. But her father, in the depths of his sickness, couldn't show his love to her. I felt like an ineffectual magician, trying to conjure the illusion of a loving father.

That first visit was uncomfortable, with its stilted small talk, but we got through it and returned to our nightly ritual of bath, books, and bed. As we snuggled together, my daughter's freshly shampooed hair tickled my nose while we read the book she'd chosen, *Lilly's Purple Plastic Purse*. She ignored *Dinosaurs Divorce*, which I'd added to her library after the separation. Lizzie studied the pictures of Lilly the mouse in her cowboy boots and demanded I reread it as soon as we got to the end. She seemed happy. Was it because she'd seen her father or because she was glad the visit was over? I wished I could read her mind as easily as I read her picture books.

Since that first dinner, visits are sporadic, as is contact between Mike and Lizzie. He rarely calls on her birthday—or anytime—unless his manic impulses make him do so over and over, as if he's determined to make up for months of neglect in one frenzied week. The episodes begin with nonstop calling, and when I finally have to just let voice mail pick up, a letter-writing campaign follows. When he's like this, I desperately hope the missives arrive while Lizzie is at school. I give her all the mail I can, but if a letter is too bizarre (and when he's manic, many are), I stash it away in a drawer. I don't throw anything out. I'm not sure what to do with these documents. I haven't decided if I'll give them to her when she's older or if I'll hide them in a trunk in the attic. Whenever a letter does make its way to her, she sometimes spirits it away into her room and other times she'll glance at it and then ignore it, leaving it on the kitchen counter until it's packed into the recycling. She doesn't want it, but she doesn't want to be the one who throws it away, either.

Lizzie's ninth birthday passed with no call from Mike. There was another hospitalization, longer this time, with mandatory clinic visits and monitored medication. It was after that that his mother called to arrange another visitation. She assured me he was better than she'd seen in a long time. Over the years, every "better" has evaporated as soon as he quits his drugs. I've steeled myself for the inevitable, concerned only how it will affect my daughter. But what if he really stays on his meds this time and wants to be more involved? Do I actually want that? The "good parent" in me says of course, but I also want Lizzie to be insulated against inconsistency, raised in a happy, secure bubble where all the people in her life are dependable and loving. Although Lizzie understands that there are surprises in life—a snow day canceling a much anticipated playdate, for example—she needs to know her parents will wake up the exact same people they were when they tucked her in bed last night and that she can always rely on them. Mike has yo-yoed into and out of her life, for her entire life. Is that fair? Of course not. It's impossible to figure out what is "fair"—I want to be so to Mike as Lizzie's father, but I want even more to protect her.

* * *

I'm not sure what Lizzie considers Mike to be—father, stranger, or something in between. But she does have a dad in her life. She has a warm and loving relationship with Jeff, and he is there for her every day. A few days before the upcoming visit, I listened as Jeff paused during his nightly story. He asked Lizzie how she felt about going to see her father. Lizzie, voice unsure, said she felt weird—she didn't know Mike and hadn't seen him for a long time—but she didn't want him to die from his sickness. Jeff tried to assure her that Mike would be okay. He told her whatever she felt was fine—if she wasn't excited to see Mike, that was okay, and if she was, that was all right, too. "You know, if you're thrilled to see Mike, my feelings won't be hurt—I love you so much," he said. I could almost hear Lizzie's exhaling relief from the other room.

We saw Mike a few days later in another town similar to where we'd met the year before. Holding hands with Lizzie and hiking through the slush to the restaurant where we were to meet, I felt my stomach spiral with dread. I studied her profile but couldn't tell how she felt. She saw me, looked up, and smiled. I squeezed her hand.

At the restaurant, Lizzie chose the seat across the table from me. Mike and his mother arrived and walked up the steps to our table. Mike's face was rounder than it had been the year before, and his beard was almost entirely gray. He looked the best I'd seen him in years—perhaps since Lizzie was a toddler. He asked her about school, inquiring what her favorite classes were and which books she enjoyed reading. He leaned in to hear her answers. Dread was replaced with doubt—maybe I'd been wrong; maybe he was ready to be involved in Lizzie's life. I felt a surge of optimism—he was better! They'd finally have a relationship! But did I want that? Did I put my daughter at risk?

Later, as I drove home, I turned down the music and glanced into the rearview mirror at Lizzie. "How do you feel?" I asked cautiously, trying to steer only the car, not the conversation.

"I feel fine, Mom," she said, fiddling with her iPod, determined to get a virtual ball in a virtual hole.

"About seeing . . ." I paused, unsure whether I should call him "Mike" or "your father."

"Mike." I cringed, certain I'd chosen the wrong noun.

"Weird, but okay. I just got annoyed when he kept putting french fries on my plate after I told him I didn't want any."

I'd noticed but hadn't said anything.

"And he gave me baby books." She was a bit miffed that she, a kid who churned through the Harry Potter and Inkheart series, had been given books for early readers.

"I know you've already read those," I commiserated, "but he was trying. We can exchange them for books you haven't read yet."

Was I validating her discomfort or insulting her father's taste in gifts? I gripped the wheel harder.

"I can't wait to see Jeff," she said, gazing out the window at frozen apple orchards.

I kept silent. I couldn't, either.

* * *

That night, after Lizzie was tucked into bed, I looked for some photos to send to Mike. I wanted him to see how the ten-year-old he'd had lunch with had grown over the years. As I sifted through my digital library, I gathered a scrapbook: a three-year-old furiously riding a tricycle, sprayed pink hair peeking from under her helmet; a five-year-old, fingers in mouth, standing nervously next to her kindergarten teacher on the first day of school; an eight-year-old costumed for her Egyptian birthday party. He'd missed so much of Lizzie's life. He was getting photos, but not the memories that went with them—it was devastatingly sad. I hit SEND, e-mailing a missed childhood.

"WHERE'S THE REST OF THIS DRESS?"

One weekend afternoon on a rare trip to the mall, Lizzie reached for one of the teal dresses that hung on the clothing carousel.

"Ew! It's missing the back!" she said, horrified. She let it drop as if it were made from battery acid rather than some sort of cottony blend fabric. The dress swung on its hanger, mocking and backless.

We had just entered not only a store in the mall but also the wide world of junior fashions. At thirteen, Lizzie had finally outgrown the kids' stores and was somewhat reluctantly shopping in juniors.

"These clothes are so dark and depressing. I like happy colors," she said, glancing tentatively around the boutique. And she does, often pairing colors that make her outfits look a bit like the flag of a small, developing country. In the store, Lizzie had been lured to the bright colors, the teals, purples, and yellows, like a moth to a flame, only to be cruelly burned by finding half the dress she expected.

It seemed that the only outfits in the place that had the colors she liked were backless, sleeveless, or extremely low cut. And Lizzie favors longer skirts and high-cut shirts—

properties not usually associated with junior fashions. Sometimes she'll find a compromise—wearing leggings with shorter skirts. I realize that by the time I finish this essay, her tastes may have changed. She's already becoming more interested in clothes shopping, while a year or so ago she'd rather have done pretty much anything else. Looking for new outfits was as much fun to her as pulling on yellow latex gloves and scrubbing the bathtub. Given her choice, she'd much rather go to the bookstore than to the mall. And I'm with her there, except that sometimes it's necessary to buy clothing, especially after yet another growth spurt that has left her with jeans that hit the high-water mark and shirts that show off her belly whenever she raises her hand.

Lizzie seems to have inherited my lack of fashion sense. In fact, we appear to be fashion senseless. I'm trying to find a happy middle ground, letting Lizzie choose her attire but occasionally suggesting gently that perhaps the lime-green corduroy miniskirt might be better paired with something other than a chartreuse shirt and fuzzy blue-and-emerald-striped socks. I want her to select her own clothing, at the store and at home, but I also want to make sure she isn't on the receiving end of the appalled stares that I experienced all too often, especially in my first days of middle school.

* * *

When we moved back to southern Louisiana from Indonesia a few weeks before I started seventh grade, my mom took my sister and me to Sears so we could each select a coat, a piece of clothing we hadn't needed the previous three years. I fell in love with a long coat made from some sort of fuzzy blue material that had a fake fur collar with blue highlights. Blue was (and still is) my favorite color.

Therefore it was perfect! Perfect, that is, had I been a pimp. My mom didn't say anything. Perhaps she was trying to let me assert my independence and newfound identity as a seventh-grade fashion casualty. Or maybe she thought it was a lovely coat and I'd made a fine choice.

Not surprisingly, middle school was my fashion nadir. I dressed for the first day of seventh grade in a blue batik wraparound skirt, red PROPERTY OF THE MACADAMIA NUT FACTORY T-shirt (we'd stopped in Hawaii on our way back to the United States), and white patent-leather shoes with a small heel that I'd picked out myself at Buster Brown. That morning, I sat on the floor of the gym, knees tucked under me for what seemed like hours, as our names were called one by one. As we were summoned, we gathered in clusters with our new homeroom teacher and then followed her to the classroom. When my name was called, I distinctly remember the clip-clop sounds my shoes made on the polished wooden gym floor as I walked in front of everyone, in a new school, in a new town, in a new country. I realized my clothing was totally wrong—all the other girls were wearing tight Chic jeans; skinny, stretchy gold belts; and Candie's or platform shoes with wooden heels, and I was certain they were staring at me. Not that they were so stylish, all dressed the same, with their hair lacquered with hair spray. They'd painted their faces, eyelids bright blue with Maybelline, lashes thick with mascara, cheeks rouged as if they'd just popped inside after a cold afternoon spent on the slopes. As I clip-clip-clopped toward my seventh-grade teacher, I kept my bare face down, reddened only from shame. I felt like a freak and wanted to look like every other seventh-grade girl in my school. I realize that they weren't all dressed identically—but to middle school me, I felt like a Troll doll in a sea of Barbies.

But how do we help young teens feel comfortable not just in their own skin, but also in their own skintight jeans or fuzzy blue coats? I don't want Lizzie to imitate her classmates' style, but I don't want her to feel like the fashion reject I perceived myself to be in middle school. I want to help balance her tastes, letting her choose her own clothing but gently editing it if her choices clash or I'm certain will elicit snickers from her classmates. It's a fine line because I also want to make sure not to tread on what she values. When she was in kindergarten and early elementary school, she mismatched proudly, as did many of her classmates. I don't want her to think I don't appreciate her choices, such as the red-bibbed prairie dress she fell in love with at a vintage clothing store but wore only once because a few kids told her that she looked like Mrs. Beasley. It's tricky, though. When she tried on the prairie dress in the store, she spun around in the mirror, smiling broadly. It was obvious she was enamored of it—and I was conflicted. Should I buy it for her? Or should I gently suggest she might want to keep looking? I bought it. Did I make the right decision?

There was a child at my daughter's school who, in seventh grade, not only appeared to be seriously into fashion, but seemed to favor clothing that could only be described as "haute hooker." She might be the nicest and most selfless girl in the world, one who spends her weekends volunteering in animal shelters and donates all of her allowance to nonprofits intent on eradicating childhood hunger, but I found it hard to get past the postage-stamp-size tight black skirt, tank top, fishnet stockings, and heels so high that there was no way she could ever play tag. And hardly even walk.

Did her parents notice her clothing? I assume they must have, since they dropped her off at school wearing those outfits. Or were they letting her assert her individuality?

Did they drive her to the mall and pull out their credit cards to buy these outfits for her? Did she try them on in front of her mother? Had she converted with zeal to the less than modest industry known as junior fashions—the same field of business that had foisted the backless dress that Lizzie and I had found in the mall when looking for more modest clothing? Perhaps she'd fallen hard for the styles the clothing companies were pushing. And it does sometimes feel a little as though they're pushing—drugs. ("Come here, little girl, and see all the microminis I've got. Try one, you'll like it. I know you want it. This time, for you, fifty percent off!")

I know there's a line between fashion sense and good sense, and between a parent letting a child find her own look and being too protective, but, as parents, we have a say. We're the ones with the credit cards and cars to drive to the store. And we get to say no when something isn't appropriate.

But then, maybe this girl's parents had decided not to fight this battle; perhaps they knew that she would come to realize on her own not only how ridiculous she looked, but how incredibly impractical her clothing choices were. Back in seventh grade, I came to realize on my own the clothing I'd selected looked absurd. Then again, I didn't show a lot of skin in white patent-leather shoes and my fuzzy blue pimp coat.

Now that Lizzie is interested in clothes and using outfits to make a statement about who she is, she's searching for her own style, riffling through carousels for her evolving identity. I do wish juniors had more and different choices beyond the backless teal dresses of their world; that there was more of a middle ground. Often it seems that young teens leapfrog from Gap Kids to Forever 21 with nothing in between. And sometimes even the children's stores offer choices that seem less than wholesome. Back when Lizzie was in fifth grade, when she was still selecting outfits in children's stores, I took her to buy her first bra. I'd planned to wait until she was in sixth grade, but the T-shirts that were popular that year were made from some sort of Lycra-cotton blend that was so gossamer thin, it showed everything even when there wasn't much to show.

"Can we look in Justice?" Lizzie said, naming her then favorite boutique.

"Sure," I said as we walked through the mall to the store, where loud pop assaulted my ears and bright colors, my eyes. Lizzie smiled, until we saw the table in the back that held the undergarments.

"This is so embarrassing," Lizzie said as I followed her to the table. She circled the surface that was piled with brightly colored padded bras. Some looked as if they belonged on an African safari, with their cheetah and tiger prints. The bras seemed to come with their very own cleavage—just add prepubescent!

"What do you think?" I said, trying to suppress my shock at bras that seemed more appropriate for older teens. Like nineteen-year-olds.

"They're . . . interesting," Lizzie said, adding, "Maybe I don't really need a bra after all."

I picked up one that looked a bit like a sports bra. It was the sole selection that was plain and had no liner. I asked what she thought.

"Well, maybe I'll try that on," she said, passing up the light blue one I was holding and grabbing the white training bra. "This one is much more me."

She tried it on and we bought two of them. Or rather, I did. Lizzie went and rummaged through T-shirts, since bra buying was "too embarrassing."

"THEY'RE HAVING TRYOUTS NEXT WEEK!"

The pool was filled with children oblivious to the chilly fall weather as they swam lap after lap. I zipped up my fleece pullover and watched as Jeff and a few other parents huddled nearby, chatting. Finally, a whistle sounded and the nonstop splashing stopped. Swim team tryouts were over.

Lizzie padded over to me, clutching a towel tossed across her shoulders like a magician's cape. Her wet hug smelled faintly of chlorine. Though her skin was speckled with goose bumps, she was grinning.

"Can I join—please?" Lizzie pleaded.

And, like that, she was on a team.

* * *

I blame the Olympics. A few weeks earlier, we'd watched the games over multiple evenings, our family sprawled together on the sofa as we fast-forwarded through to our favorite events, mostly swimming, diving, and gymnastics.

Lizzie was fascinated by the swimming competition, and

since she knew that I was on a swim team as a teenager, she showered me with questions:

"What was your favorite stroke, Mom?"

"What were swim meets like?"

"Could you do what they're doing in the Olympics?"

(Yeah sure. I'll just dust off all the gold medals I've got stashed in the coat closet.)

Earlier that summer, she'd been to sleepaway camp and had spent afternoons distance swimming in a cold Vermont lake. One day she swam three miles and was rightfully proud. Her camp is a very crunchy, noncompetitive girl-power kind of place where they celebrate special events like "Amazing Woman Day." Her long-distance swimming was to challenge herself, not to compete against anyone else. Now she was captivated by team swimming. I watched her study the swimmers as if they were the answer to a previously unknown question, her jaw slightly agape.

Because I know the monumental commitment year-round swimming takes for both the swimmer and her family, I've never pushed it. Actually, I've never forced any sport. I felt that an interest in sports—or any other activity—had to come from Lizzie. Plus, I enjoy my weekends free. But the Olympics triggered something, and Lizzie's genuine interest was impossible to ignore.

She'd been on a casual, noncompetitive team for a few years, one that met once a week, more for the social and exercise aspects than anything else. But it wasn't satisfying to her.

"I like it, but there's only one meet—and you compete against your teammates. That's kind of lame," she said.

I understood what she meant. A noncompetitive swim team *is* kind of lame. She saw through the "Everyone's a winner" mentality and decided it was a con. It sucks the thrill out of being part of a team—a real one, with its winning and losing, one where cheering for teammates or having them yell for her actually means something. And when losing isn't an option, the sweet taste of victory can be aspartame-artificial.

In preschool, Lizzie ran a race where everyone got "first" ribbons. About a dozen four- to six-year-olds, dressed in shorts, T-shirts, and sneakers, stood behind a chalk mark on a high school field one spring morning a half hour before an adult 5K race was due to start.

A man in his fifties, wearing a striped referee shirt, yelled, "Ready, set, go!" Off the kids went, running toward the finish line fifty yards down the field, where a beaming woman held a bouquet of green ribbons, which she gave to each runner as he or she finished the race. The ribbon read, "Number 1." Lizzie ran as fast as her four-year-old legs would carry her. She was passed by some runners and beat others. When Lizzie reached the finish line and the woman gave her the ribbon, she burst into tears.

"I didn't win!" she whimpered, clenching her ribbon and hiccuping through her sobs. She was upset because she didn't come in first and because everyone had received the same consolation prize. Even then, she knew that the ribbon had no meaning.

I'm conflicted. I like the concept of sports for fun and believe it's important for Lizzie to be both a good winner and a good loser, but some sports teams are far too serious— and that's not what I want for my daughter. As a parent, I wanted to find that happy middle ground for my daughter between "noncompetitive" and too competitive.

It was a few weeks after Missy Franklin's final Olympic swim that we found ourselves at that busy pool, along with a few dozen other parents whose kids undoubtedly saw themselves as future Missy Franklins or Michael Phelpses.

Lizzie had found out about the team tryouts by doing some research on her iPod.

"Look, I found a year-round team. And tryouts are in a few weeks. Can I go?" Lizzie said, holding the tiny screen up to me. I squinted. It was difficult to make out the words without my glasses.

I had to think for a few minutes.

We're not a team sports kind of family—or Lizzie and I are not. (My husband played on a baseball team as recently as a few years ago.) We run and participate in races, but Lizzie hasn't shown much interest over the years in organized athletics. There have been brief flings with them, however. There was peewee soccer, with five-year-olds and their overeager parents perched on the edges of their folding chairs at the high school's athletic field, shouting as if it were a World Cup semifinal. Lizzie played one season of "competitive" soccer during fifth grade that involved far more high fives than goals.

"Look at her play!" Lizzie said one weekend night as she reclined on the floor in front of our television, her arms folded under her chin, watching a DVD of *Bend It Like Beckham*. "Our school's team isn't quite that good. Yet."

She developed a take-it-or-leave-it view of soccer. Mostly she left it, although back in kindergarten she quite took to the uniform and occasionally wore her shin guards around the house.

Lizzie also comes from a line of humans more likely to run from a ball than catch it. Along with attached earlobes and an ability to roll my tongue, I have passed the klutz gene to her. In elementary school phys ed, we often played cabbage ball, a softball-like game with a regular bat and bigger, softer ball. I was always placed in far left field— really far and really left. That way, I was pretty safe from any wayward cabbage ball. But if one was hit in my direction, I ran the other way. Back in middle school, my volleyballs never volleyed. They smacked loudly against my hand, leaving a red welt before they bounced limply a few times on the shiny wooden gym floor.

Then I found swim team. In an attempt to have some sort of social life, I joined my neighborhood team the summer between seventh and eighth grade and found I liked it. I rode my three-speed Schwinn bike the mile to the pool each morning before the dew evaporated in the July heat. Jumping into that cool water, I escaped from more than the already oppressive humidity—the steady back-and-forth in the lanes took me far away from my small southern town. The few swim meets we had gave me an excuse to be around other kids my age. In the fall, I continued on our town's newly formed year-round team. I was terrible. I slapped the water as if it were a cad and I were its jilted lover. But I enjoyed it and kept working. It was a chance to be part of a team, but independent at the same time. No one would get angry and sarcastically mutter, "Nice job," if I swam a hundred-yard backstroke badly. The team, perhaps because it was new or maybe because of the time, was competitive, but not cutthroat. Swimmers varied drastically in their abilities, and all were welcomed and encouraged.

After our team's first season, there was an awards ceremony. Trophies were given to the most valuable team member and, in each age group, to the fastest swimmers. I applauded politely as child after child left the table to collect gleaming trophies. Then, to my surprise, my name was called. I walked slowly to where Coach Kelly was holding a big trophy, took it, and shook his hand. I felt so proud! I was "Most Improved." I'd improved to the point that I was no longer terrible—just awful. I held the trophy tightly on the ride home, studying the little golden swimmer on top who was about to dive and running my finger over the plaque.

Once home, I put it on my desk. I kept swimming. Over time, I started placing and even winning races. The lonely swimmer on the trophy became less so. My desk filled with trophies and my room with medals and ribbons, which I stuck to a large cork bulletin board. I cut out photos from our local paper's sports page of swim meets and pinned those, too. My room was becoming a shrine to swimming, and I did all but offer up a sacrifice to the god of chlorine.

* * *

After team tryouts, Lizzie was placed in a group that met each day after school. Her first practice, she stood in a huddle with the other children while the coach spoke to them.

"Okay, into the pool!" he shouted.

Lizzie hopped into a lane with what looked to be other young teens. She smiled shyly at another girl and I could see them chatting until they started swimming laps. Later, during that first practice, Jeff and I sat on a metal bench and watched children working with kickboards. Lizzie and the girl from earlier stayed side by side, talking as much as they kicked. There were many different levels, from newly minted swimmers to serious, dedicated kids in the far lane. The coach, in sweats and the short hairstyle favored by members of the military and coaches everywhere, watched over the swimmers and answered parents' questions.

"This is giving me a bad feeling. I'm having flashbacks," Jeff said quietly, shuddering slightly while watching the coach. Back in middle school, his tennis coach hated him because he did things his own way. While everyone else on the team employed the usual backhand and forehand, Jeff would just toss the racket from one hand to another, giving himself two forehands. The coach became increasingly unhappy when Jeff kept beating his favorites on the team during competitions. Jeff's organized athletic career came to a screeching halt when his mother gave him and his brother two matinee tickets to see *Hair* on Broadway.

The coach saw an opening. "If you miss practice, you're off the team." Fourteen-year-old Jeff thought about it for a minute: tennis team or a gaggle of beautiful naked dancers right in front of him on the stage.

"Coach—this is the dawning of the Age of Aquarius."

❋　❋　❋

Both Jeff and I have triggers that cause us to time travel right back to middle school. I'm whisked there when Lizzie is on the receiving end of mean-girl activity. At swim practice, I learned coaches take Jeff to a time of rebellion and protest against anyone with authority.

Although Lizzie's coach had a great way of speaking to the children, firm yet supportive, Jeff's comments while we watched the coach direct the kids made me pause. Although I grew up a decade after Jeff, in an era that didn't overly challenge authority and in a place (the Deep South) that actually embraced it, I still have conflicted feelings about authority figures.

As parents, we teach our children to obey authority, in the form of parents, teachers, or coaches. But is that necessarily a good thing? When can blind obedience benefit from a trip to the optometrist and a new pair of glasses? Will our children feel fine disregarding rules and those in charge if something makes them squeamish? Back when I was on swim team, our coach's word was golden. We did whatever he told us to do, whether it was jumping into a freezing pool or running several miles around neighborhood streets. We huddled at swim meets, focusing on what he said as if he were an oracle, determined to earn the elusive, "Nice job." He never gave us any reason not to trust him.

Though Lizzie doesn't hesitate to tell us when something makes her uncomfortable, she loves rules. And although that makes for a generally obedient adolescent, for which even agnostic parents would get down on their knees and thank God in gratitude, is there a way to help infuse her respect for authority with a healthy dose of skepticism? She wants to do well on the team. Does she have to obey all authority to succeed?

I don't have the answer. Lizzie has been practicing with her new team for three months and is motivated. She's okay with not being the fastest and works harder to be better. She's fitting in and feels she's a valued part of the team. She's already participated in three swim meets.

"Look at this button I got at practice today!" she said, pointing to a small one that she'd pinned to her practice bag. Beside the name of the team, it read, "Personal Best." During her second meet, she'd beat her time for her first hundred-yard freestyle by five seconds.

She held up the button so I could better see it.

"Next meet, I want to try and get another—I'm going to work superhard at practice so I can beat my time again!"

And she did. At her third meet, she earned another button.

I hope she can find balance: between being competitive, but not overly so; between respecting authority, but not blindly; between working hard at practice and having fun. I have to trust that she'll find the equilibrium, even if she sees Jeff wincing every time the coach barks an order. For now, if she wants to be part of a team and as long as she continues to enjoy it, we'll be there for her. Especially since families are required to volunteer.

"WILL THE WORLD BE AROUND WHEN I HAVE KIDS?"

Our family sat around the polished wooden dining table one night, discussing the day's events at school and in the news. We'd put the dinner plates in the dishwasher, and Lizzie had helped me scoop chocolate ice cream into little glass bowls. A front-page story in that day's *New York Times* about climate change, and a review of Mark Hertsgaard's book *Hot: Living Through the Next Fifty Years on Earth* about how it was already well under way, had steered our conversation from school to this more sober direction.

"Will the world be around when I have kids?" Lizzie asked. She put her spoon down and looked at us, her eyes filled with worry.

I was momentarily filled with guilt about causing Lizzie anxiety. But we've always, in an age-appropriate way, discussed news events with her. We don't watch television news, but there have always been newspapers lying around. (We still get our local paper delivered, although we subscribe to others digitally.) We think it's important for Lizzie to know what's going on in the world.

Jeff assured her that, yes, the world would be around, but climate change might make it a very different place, especially by the time her children had children.

"But your generation can help find a way to make things better!" I said, overly brightly. I have to be honest about climate change—I can't candy-coat reality—but I want there to be hope, too. I don't want bleak images of more frequent and severe weather events, melting polar ice caps, rising seas, and famines dancing nonstop in her head. Jeff told Lizzie that studying science (her current plans for college) is a good way to find solutions. He told her that kids her age will, literally, help to save the world when they're older.

"It's so scary," she said, playing with a frayed thread on her place mat. We agreed that it was.

There have always been frightening future-shattering events that children see on television, read in newspapers, or hear about from others. Since kids often don't fully understand them, they can lodge like a splinter in their imaginations, causing worry.

"Are our friends in New York City okay?" Lizzie asked after reading about Hurricane Sandy's devastation. "My friends in New Paltz and Massachusetts are fine—they said they got to miss school."

I assured her that our friends were safe. Lizzie looked relieved.

"I don't like climate change," she said.

* * *

I grew up with the threat of global communism. The domino theory promised governments would tumble, one after the other, until our country was run by evil-looking men dressed in ill-fitting gray suits and twirling thick mustaches, intent on enslaving us. We would all (children included) work five-year plans in the People's Factory, where the foremen spoke like Boris and Natasha on *The Rocky & Bullwinkle Show*.

As my sister and I ate our Libbyland TV dinners from their compartmentalized aluminum trays on the kitchen table, we could hear our television blathering on in the background as our parents watched the news. And it was all about Vietnam. Men in camouflage raced around in a faraway land. The news anchor informed us, between our Tater Tots and chocolate pudding, that the war was to stop communism from coming our way. Occasionally, the news would cut to a shot of protesters. This caused my dad to leap from the sofa and shout at the screen. So I learned communism was bad and protesters were worse.

My husband was in elementary school during the Cuban missile crisis. In second grade, he and his classmates marched from their classroom in an orderly line behind their teacher. Out in the hallway, they obediently sat on the floor and tucked their heads between their legs. That way, they were told, if an atom bomb was dropped near their suburban Long Island school, their faces would be protected. From this, Jeff learned adults were not always honest.

It's not only geopolitical events that can terrify children. When our family moved back to the United States from Indonesia, it was the summer of both the bicentennial and Legionnaires' disease. My sister and I sat, cross-legged, on the shag carpet of my grandmother's suburban Washington, DC, apartment, transfixed by the Saturday morning cartoons. *Scooby-Doo* gave way to news of a mysterious illness that was killing people in Philadelphia. I was certain that, since that city was sort of close to where we now sat watching television, we'd catch it, too, and I wouldn't live long enough to find out what life as a middle schooler was like.

The point is, kids often don't have a filter to ferret the truth from hype. The chances that anyone in our family would contract Legionnaires' disease was pretty much nonexistent, and even if I were to have caught it somehow, there was little likelihood it would have killed me. But according to my twelve-year-old interpretation of the network news, I was a goner.

It's overwhelming for a child to wrap her mind around something terrifying, whether it's climate change, an epidemic, or war. They have to be able to picture a way out—it's like they need a mental escape hatch. Since, as a kid, Lizzie has no real power, she needs to believe she can help solve climate problems.

* * *

I built my own mental escape hatch as a child. When I was eleven, we stopped in Denmark one summer on our way back to the United States. After the Little Mermaid statue and open-faced sandwiches, we visited the Resistance Museum. I knew about Nazis and the Holocaust. I'd read Anne Frank's diary and had seen her house in Amsterdam earlier on the same trip. But being in the museum and seeing photos of those who were there was different. The shock of the photographs, of seeing people who threw themselves on the electrified fence to die rather than face the wretched conditions and slow death, was far more vivid than words alone. We saw shoes with false heels for smuggling food into the camps.

"We'd run away and hide in the woods," I told my parents. "We'd have shoes like those so we could smuggle food." I was certain enough food for us all would fit in that one square inch of space. It had to.

I had a plan! It was almost as if my child's mind needed a safe place. I couldn't fathom the horror of what life must have been like, especially when it was all too brief and involved children. I needed a fairyland of a forest where everyone was safe and warm and had enough to eat.

* * *

The night we discussed climate change after dinner, once Lizzie heard that she could help find solutions, she visibly relaxed. She now had her own fairyland forest. Except that hers isn't necessarily a fairy tale. If Lizzie continues to be interested in studying science, perhaps she will one day help find answers to today's very real problems. I wouldn't be surprised. After all, she's been fascinated by the environment for a long time, starting back in second grade, when she first learned about the Earth's changing climate. Her teacher mentioned melting ice caps and potentially drowning polar bears one day during current events. According to her teacher, it elicited this response from Lizzie:

"Nooooooooooooooooooooooooooooooooooooo!"

That day, Lizzie decided, on her own, to donate $5 of her money to save the polar bears.

After we'd talked about finding answers to climate change, as Lizzie licked the last bit of ice cream from her spoon and placed it in the little bowl, she looked at us, eyes sparkling.

"I just know scientists will help the world be safe for my kids' kids," she said, and paused. She added, "And maybe you'll meet them—maybe scientists will discover a way to make people live a long time."

I'll get my walker ready.

"I'm making
a list."

"Of what?"

One morning on our way to school, I slammed the car door after our goldendoodle, Wally, had jumped into the backseat, ready for his morning ride. I got behind the wheel as Lizzie crawled into the passenger seat, clutching her notebook and a pen. I enjoy these mundane car trips. They're a chance to chat about whatever is on our minds or to simply zone out quietly together.

"I'm making a list," Lizzie said, and flipped open the notebook on her lap. She scribbled something on the paper.

"Of what?" I asked. Lizzie was constantly jotting things in her notebook. Poems. Drawings. Character ideas for her novel or other stories.

"Of some of the things I want to try and do during my life," she said, looking over at me.

I have trouble deciding which items to add to the grocery list.

"Do you want to hear what I just added?" she asked, holding up the notebook.

Of course I did.

"Make a difference in the world," she said. "Do you want to hear the other stuff I want to do?"

I did. But first I had to blink back my tears of maternal pride.

Lizzie rattled off goals from her list.

"Of course, I won't do all these right away," she assured me.

Our car trips have been full of surprises. Since Lizzie and I aren't looking directly at each other (I want to be sure I don't go barreling off the road), our conversations have allowed us to discover all sorts of things—and we've found it's sometimes easier to talk if we're not gazing into each other's eyes. Over recent years, we've talked about drugs, both her knowledge of them ("I know what a weed brownie is!") and her innocence about them, as evidenced when she sang along to a Rodriguez song, changing the lyrics from drugs to clothing ("jumpers, coats, and sweet Mary Janes"). I've learned what she values in a boy-crush. ("I like him because he's nice and smart. And he's funny, too. And cute.") Our conversations are usually pleasurable, although sometimes she uses this time to bring up things that are bothering her, like those occasions when she's felt left out in school.

The list was one of those pleasant surprises. It grew out of one of Lizzie's seventh-grade classes, where they had been discussing their goals for the school year. Lizzie took the assignment very seriously and ran with it. It quickly acquired a life of its own and became a list of life goals. She was taking her notebook to school to share them with a friend.

* * *

Recently, I asked her if she still had the list and whether she might share it for this book. She was very pleased to do so.

"Maybe other kids can start their own," she said.

List of Things I Want to Do in My Life
by Lizzie

- ❏ become an astronaut and see outer space
- ❏ write a complete novel
- ❏ get something published
- ❏ travel abroad for a year
- ❏ become a great musician
- ❏ go horseback riding
- ❏ be in a play
- ❏ become fluent in a different language
- ❏ be a teacher
- ❏ help bring change, by organizing it
- ❏ have chickens
- ❏ grow a garden
- ❏ fill up an entire notebook with stuff
- ❏ make a book into a secret place for hiding things
- ❏ read 10,000 books
- ❏ go camping
- ❏ climb a mountain
- ❏ research something for fun
- ❏ graduate into a good college and grad school
- ❏ go in a tree house
- ❏ go zip-lining
- ❏ have daydreams
- ❏ see moose
- ❏ try frog legs
- ❏ have a British tea
- ❏ see the Olympics
- ❏ go to the Harry Potter Museum
- ❏ play tennis
- ❏ win a race in a swim meet
- ❏ solve a mystery
- ❏ ride a boat in a lake

- ❏ memorize a poem and song
- ❏ play the violin
- ❏ be a counselor at my summer camp
- ❏ make a difference in the world

There are goals she is already well on the way to achieving and ones that, as she reminded me in the car, might take a while. Hearing her goals made me ponder my own. I didn't have a collection of lofty and less so plans when I was her age.

✳ ✳ ✳

I learned a lot from Lizzie's list. It made me wonder whether I could put my own together, even if its entries would be notably less ambitious than hers.

Mine might include writing every day, whether I feel like it or not; not letting unimportant details weigh me down; taking a walk each day; planning a relaxing, do-nothing family vacation in the not too distant future; singing out loud in the car without embarrassment; going on more date nights with Jeff; cheering loudly at swim meets, but not jumping up and down wildly; being less judgmental of myself; and going hiking more frequently in the Columbia River Gorge.

Sometimes, as parents we forget we need to maintain our own list of goals, outside of raising our kids.

Lizzie's list also drove home a reminder that so much of being a parent is not about teaching and talking to your child; it's about learning from and listening to them. And helping them reach for their goals: I found a restaurant in Portland that serves traditional British afternoon tea and we recently went.

"To reaching goals," I said to Lizzie, holding out my cup to hers.

"Goals are delicious!" Lizzie said, clinking cups and popping a tiny cucumber sandwich into her mouth.

ACKNOWLEDGMENTS

Thank you to the talented and thoughtful people at The Experiment, especially Cara Bedick, who, after reading one of my essays, took a chance on me. She's an editor extraordinaire. Thank you also to Molly Cavanaugh, Jack Palmer, and, of course, Matthew Lore.

This book came about in part because Sarah Hepola at *Salon* found an essay of mine in the e-slush pile and decided to run it. That led to Cara reading it and contacting me.

Thank you also to Candace Walsh, who published one of my first personal essays and gave me the confidence to continue. Thank you also to Judy Goldberg and Barbara Brandon-Croft at *Parents*; Celia Shatzman at *Family Circle*; Marcelle Soviero, Honor Jones, Mira Jacob, Isaac Fitzgerald, Jack Murnighan, and Alison Brower.

Mark Levine, an expert in the field, was kind enough to help me decipher the publishing contract. Jeff Kisseloff read early versions of the essays (and reread and reread) and gave me valuable suggestions. Family and friends who offered help and answered countless questions included Robert and Barbara Sanders, Laura Sanders, assorted Sanders and Kisseloffs, Julia and Kate Fishman, Cathy and Kelvin Ono, Melissa Holbrook Pierson, Clare Allen Wang, David and Terry Cohen, Brianne Williams, Alise Loebelsohn, Sara Karlen, the Moes, Ed Kowalachuk, Lisa Hill, Margaret Foley, Nancy and Sarah Edwards, Samantha Waltz, Bethany Rohde, Lori Estrada, Shari Perott, Michelle Hernandez, Heidi Hillery, Michelle Miller, Gnanse Nelson, Lesa Myrick, Mary Beth Bobeck Muir, Heather Bell Atria, Kitty Caromdy Hagan, Anne Phipps, and Erin Moore, who was especially helpful. Thank you also to the teachers and staff at Lizzie's school and summer camp.

The best parts of this book are the results of their invaluable input.